RAFFI

(Hagob Melik Hagobian, cir. 1835-1888)

THE GOLDEN ROOSTER

translated from the original Armenian
and introduced by
Donald Abcarian

Gomidas Institute
London

This publication is dedicated to Djivan and Mariam

GOMIDAS INSTITUTE - ARMENIAN LITERATURE IN TRANSLATION

Originally published by Taderon Press in association with the Gomidas Institute.

New edition, Gomidas Institute, 2021.

© 2008 Donald Abcarian. All Rights Reserved.

ISBN 978-1-909382-58-9

Gomidas Institute
42 Blythe Rd.
London, W14 0HA
ENGLAND
Email: *info@gomidas.org*
Web: *www.gomidas.org*

TABLE OF CONTENTS

ABOUT THE AUTHOR

Raffi (né Hakob Melik-Hakobian) was born in 1835 in Bayajuk, near Salmas, in northwestern Persia. He died in Tiflis in 1888. He was a prolific and popular writer who contributed to Krikor Ardzrouni's Tiflis-based liberal periodical, *Mshak* (Cultivator). He is considered the greatest Armenian novelist and social commentator of the 20th century.

ABOUT THE TRANSLATOR

Donald Abcarian was born and raised in Fresno, California, where his family was part of the extensive Armenian-American community that has settled there since the turn of the last century. His earliest influences, including the Armenian language, derived from that milieu. He graduated from the University of California at Berkeley with a degree in philosophy and has pursued a lifelong interest in languages and world literature. His translations also include Raffi's *The Fool* and *Jalaleddin*.

ABOUT THE PUBLISHERS

Gomidas Institute is an independent academic organization dedicated to modern Armenian studies and research. For more information see *www.gomidas.org* or *contact info@gomidas.org*.

Introduction to the English Edition.

In Tbilisi, Georgia, 1856, with just one year left to complete his academic preparation for admission to a Russian university, Raffi received word from his ailing father that he must drop his studies and return home immediately to help run the family business. With this news his bright prospects of some day going on to a career in medicine or diplomacy came to an abrupt end and a pivotal new decade in his life began.

Raffi returned home to Salmast[1] a new man, a young intellectual who had been deeply immersed in the classics of western literature and brought back with him as one of the most treasured accomplishments of his Tbilisi years the first novel he had ever written.[2] He returned with the determination that whatever the burden of workaday responsibilities in the years to come he would never sacrifice his intellectual life or lay aside his pen. He never wavered in that determination. In pursuit of his egalitarian ideals he soon founded the first school for boys and girls in his native Salmast. A short time later he paid his first visit to Western Armenia (Van, Bitlis, Moush) and there gathered a wealth of material that he would soon draw upon to write the works that brought him his earliest recognition as an author.

But in 1865 tragedy struck. Raffi's father perished in the great cholera epidemic that swept over Salmast in that year. Overnight, Raffi's large family – once distinguished and wealthy – fell on very hard times. His father's numerous business rivals immediately descended on the family estate to pick it apart with a host of

---

1   Salmast (or Salmas) is a town and district in northwestern Iran near the northern tip of Lake Urmia. Raffi's family home was in the village of Bayajouk there.
2   This novel, originally written in Classical Armenian, was subsequently reworked into modern Armenian and published as *Salpi*.

fraudulent claims, and Raffi was forced to rush from one place to another to try salvaging enough of it to sustain his family. Despite all his efforts he failed. He and his family were reduced to abject poverty, and Raffi was compelled to take a lowly job as an accountant for a clothing shop in Tbilisi to support them. These are the experiences that lie at the core of *The Golden Rooster*.

The Golden Rooster is the second and most popular in a trilogy[3] of short novels focusing on the ethos and social significance of the traditional Armenian merchant class of the Caucasus. With this trilogy Raffi sought to 'tear away the mask of gold' covering the faces of these powerful merchants and lay bare for all to see the trickery and moral bankruptcy that was at the heart of their success. At the same time, he sought to suggest a more honorable course for a new generation of merchants, young men willing and able to make a genuine contribution to the larger interests of Armenian society.

The Golden Rooster was first published serially in Tbilisi in the newspaper *Mshag* [The Cultivator] from August to September 1879. It saw its first publication as a separate book in November 1882. Although it was thus put into final form and published after *Jalaleddin* and *The Fool*, its inception and essential character belong to the previous phase of Raffi's career, the relatively secure period that preceded the outbreak of the Russo-Turkish War of 1877. Despite the gravity of its purpose, this is what accounts for the novel's prevailing airiness and optimism and the charming representation it offers of everyday life in an Armenian town - its comings and goings, its marketplace and relations with village life, its festivities and diversions, all of which distinguishes it markedly from the stern tenor of his later works. This is a large part of its special interest. Taking these contrasting aspects of the novel into consideration, one of its most notable achievements can be seen in the remarkable balance it strikes between darkness and light.

---

3   The first is entitled *Zahroumar* [an expletive roughly equivalent to "Rubbish!"], the second and present work *Voski Akaghagh* ["The Golden Rooster"], and the last *Minn Aysbess Myusn Aynbess* [very roughly, "One's Like This The Other's Like That"].

As is usually the case with Raffi's novels, this one takes us to a completely new locale, a fictional market town deep in eastern Armenia near the western shores of Lake Sevan. Most of the story unfolds at the home and store of 'the agha', Bedros Masisian, characterized by Raffi as a 'holdover' from the wily Armenian merchants of a previous age. With probing realism Masisian's every move and thought are followed relentlessly from one end of the story to the other, from church to marketplace, from crowded store to the sweltering and unkempt solitude of his room. In describing Masisian's household, style of dress and values, Raffi brings the very flux of history before our eyes, a new era nudging the old one aside. Masisian's son, Stepan, is a representative of that future with his longing for education and liberation and the tender concern he shows for Kalo, the young apprentice whose plight is so poignantly depicted, stirring as it does with the almost palpable shadows of *Oliver Twist*.

This translation is taken from volume 3 of the 1984 edition of *The Collected Works of Raffi* published by "Sovedagan Krogh" ['The Soviet Writer'] in Yerevan, supervised, edited, and richly annotated by Dr. Khachik Samvelyan to whom much is owed.

The notation system for the story works as follows: an asterisk follows a word or term to be explained; that word or term will be found in alphabetic order at the back of the book in the section entitled "ENDNOTES". The reader should also know that the chapters titles have been added by me for dramatic focus and were not part of the original.

My heartfelt thanks go to my entire family for the gracious support and encouragement they have given me in the course of this translation.

In closing, I wish to express my sincere appreciation to Ara Sarafian and Gomidas Institute without whose steadfast presence and dedication this translation of "The Golden Rooster" would never have seen the light of day.

Donald Abcarian
Berkeley, California
February 2008

THE GOLDEN ROOSTER

PART I

Chapter 1

Kalo and His Song

There was a little boy in the village of B——— who had captured everyone's attention. He had just turned twelve years of age. The devout villagers would be enthralled by the sound of his voice as they made their way to church early each morning and passed him tending his sheep in the fields nearby and singing the sweetest of melodies.

The little boy's name was Kaloust[*] but the villagers called him Kalo for short. He was sturdy and well-built, this little Kalo, with evident reserves of physical strength. He didn't have a bad looking face, either; burnt almost black by the sun and showing incipient signs of attractive, regular features, in its midst were planted a pair of wild and fiery eyes that reflected an intensely bright disposition.

Kalo was an orphan. His parents had perished in the last great cholera outbreak and they had left him, their only child, in the bitterest poverty. He was taken in by his father's kind-hearted brother, Aved, who felt it was his sacred duty to do so and took care of him like a true father. Aved was held in very high esteem by the other villagers and for that reason was called "brother" by all. He was a steady, hardworking man and often helped to settle the various disputes that broke out among his neighbors.

Brother Aved had a small family, a household consisting of himself, his wife Yelisabet, two little children and his mother Shushan who was seventy years old and ruled the household with all the authority of her years. Elderly women are generally kind by nature, but

Shushan was especially so, and she had a special place in her heart for little Kalo in whom she found the likeness of her deceased son.

Little Kalo helped his uncle with the domestic chores for three seasons of the year, but during winter he went to study the prayer-book under a priest. To say "study" means simply that he orally memorized parts of various liturgical chants and prayers without ever truly learning to read.

Kalo's responsibilities around the house were rather light compared to the lot of most peasant children. He rose early in the morning to take a pitcher and fetch water from the spring. After that he cleaned up the yard and helped Yelisabet milk the cows. Milking cows is traditionally a girl's job, but Brother Aved had no daughters and his sons were too small for the task. If there was nothing further to do around the house, Kalo would put on his sandals, stick a piece of cracker bread in his pocket, take his shepherd's staff, which was twice his height, and drive a flock of sheep into the fields to graze. He was quite responsible in the way he behaved and was seldom threatened with being spanked by the local peasants.

Kalo was very popular with his friends, and often he and they would join all their sheep together into one large flock and drive them to graze on the banks of the Arax, which wasn't far from their village. Kalo was the joy of his comrades, springing all sorts of pranks and jokes on them, and often lightening their hours with his sweet songs or playing his reed flute, in which he had considerable proficiency. But after rescuing one of his playmates from drowning in the Arax, where they had gone for a swim, he assumed heroic standing and was respected ever after.

When his friends were ready to settle down on the grass at midday to have a modest lunch, they'd say to him, "Kalo, come and have some bread with us, you don't have a mother . . . Our mother put butter and cream on it. Come on, have some," they'd repeat.

Chapter 2

A New Day

It was one of the days in the last week of the Lenten fast. During this week the villagers would transport their commodities to town to ensure that the rich had everything they needed to have an enjoyable Easter. And so, at the rooster's first call Brother Aved got out of bed in the morning darkness, lit the lamp, washed up, then crossed himself and began to load up his donkeys. Except for Yelisabet, who was helping him, the rest of the family were still asleep. On the previous day Yelisabet had prepared a number of commodities to be taken to the market: two jugs of oil, some fresh cheese, two baskets of eggs, and a few hens.

Such prominent activities could hardly have escaped Kalo's lively attention, and at the first sound of his uncle's footsteps his head popped up from his pillow.

"You're going to take me with you. I'm coming, too," he said, opening his bright eyes wide.

"Where do you mean?" his uncle responded rather crossly.

"To town."

Despite his normally cool disposition Brother Aved had got angry about something that night and seemed quite dejected. People like that sometimes take their anger out on completely innocent objects, and Kalo became that object.

"Hush up brat! That's all I need, for you to go to town with us!" he bellowed.

Kalo fell silent. He laid his head back down on his pillow and pulled the covers over his head, crying softly to himself. He shared the bed with his grandmother and she woke up at the sounds.

"Goodness, dear, what made you cry like that?" she asked.

Kalo barely managed to tell her what had happened before Brother Aved came back in for some last minute items.

"Why make the poor boy cry, son?" Shushan asked. "He wants to go with you. Just take him along. Why break his heart?"

"This isn't the right time," said Aved, calming down a bit.

"The Bedrosian's son Kyuki is going . . . He's no older than I am," said Kalo from beneath his covers.

"Take him along, son," Shushan urged her son persuasively. "Take him so that he can see the world. He's not a girl that he has to be kept shut in, he's a boy and he wants to go. He'll learn something and his eyes will be opened."

Yelisabet spoke up in support of her mother-in-law and added that Kalo could help manage the donkey.

"All right, on your feet then and let's go. Just don't slow me down," said Aved finally.

Going to town during Easter week was a major treat to peasant children and their fathers would buy them new clothing there – cloaks, caps, sandals. Kalo was thrilled; this would be his first time to town.

He flew out of bed, already dressed as usual, and dashed about hardly knowing what he was looking for. After locating his shepherd's staff and tying on his sandals he was ready to go. He took his tall staff and went up to his grandmother.

"What shall I bring back for you, grandma?" he asked, wrapping his arm around her neck.

Her deepset eyes welled with tears and she kissed him silently.

All the donkeys were now loaded up and waiting in the yard. Yelisabet stood by while Aved went into the sheepfold. He emerged with a tiny two-month old lamb. He secured it on the load and thought to himself, "This we'll take for the agha* . . ."

The caravan set out well before sunrise.

Chapter 3

The Road Away

As Aved led his donkeys up the road he was joined by a number of other peasants who were also on their way to market and soon the caravan became quite large.

The weather was calm, the air full of delicate springtime freshness, and the stars twinkled gaily in the clear sky. Despite the recent rains the ground was dry and the donkeys could walk without getting stuck. Kalo and some of the others boys drove the donkeys while their fathers sauntered along behind engaged in conversation:

"We'll see how the flour sells," said one of the men.

"I heard the price went up," said another.

"If we can't get a good price now, then when?" interjected a third man.

"There wasn't any snow all winter and we're really going to be in a bad way this summer. We'll be lucky just to have enough water to drink."

"But that last rain really helped. Without it the fields would totally have dried up."

"What good is just one rain? Can you give a camel water with a spoon? No, the heavens have closed up because of our sins."

"The priest hasn't made his rounds with the cross and gospel yet. God may still have mercy on us," offered another peasant, crossing himself.

"Every day the priest runs to the government with his satchel of curses tucked under his arm, but every day he comes back with only new demands: 'Give us this. Give us that' after we've already given them our very souls . . . You never know whose ire you're going to come up against these days. . . They all want something . . . While we don't have a single kopeck to our name . . ."

One pious old peasant took offense at such talk: "Is that any way to talk, to say that God is angry, that He's turned his face away from us, that He's given us no snow or rain? Whatever you think of Him, our priests' prayers sustain us."

"They say the price of butter has gone up," added another man. "How much did you sell yours for, Margos?"

"Ten manets."*

"And how much for your eggs?"

"A hundred."

"That's really good!"

"What are you getting all worked up about?" said Brother Aved, finally entering into the conversation after a prolonged silence. "Whether you sell high or low, it's all the same. Take whatever you can use back with you. Men like us are nothing but serfs to the city folk. Twelve months a year we labor and plow and plant just for them. They take our flour and butter and cheese and eat it up and keep their pockets stuffed with money while we never get out of debt. We carry our produce to town but come back empty handed and have to listen shamefully to our wives and children asking us, 'So what did you bring back from town for us?'"

Brother Aved's remarks had a distinctly dampening effect on the general mood and everyone fell silent as if struck by lightning, for nothing is so depressing to a peasant as being reminded of his debts. This was the very reason Brother Aved was in such a bad mood a few hours earlier as he was loading up his donkeys. He was reflecting on how the entire load, the fruit of his sweat and heavy labor, didn't belong to him. . .

But Kalo's happy bunch, free of their parents' worries and never having received their first demand for taxes or collateral, were engaged in an altogether different kind of conversation as they drove the caravan of donkeys up the road:

"Where do the townspeople graze their sheep, Saki?" Kalo asked one of his companions.

"The town's folk don't have any sheep," responded Saki.

"Well, what do the children do all day if they don't have sheep to tend?" asked Kalo.

"They go to school."*

"How does the priest punish them when they don't learn their lessons?"

"They aren't taught by a priest. I told you, they go to a school."

"But what's a school?"

Not knowing what to say, Saki dodged the question:

"A school is a school. . . Don't you understand?"

"I'll bet you can get good sandals in town," said another boy.

"They don't wear sandals. They wear clogs," answered Saki.

"What are clogs?"

"Clogs are the kind of sandals the Russians wear."

"Do they have blackberries and medlar* fruit?" asked another boy.

"No, the forest is far from town."

"Then what do the town boys eat?"

Saki didn't know how to answer this barrage of questions except by giving his companions a brief sketch of life in town – at least as much as he himself knew. He told them that there were large houses and a market place, that instead of oxen and buffalo they used horses, but only to ride. He added that the boys who lived in town made fun of country boys and often beat them up.

Hearing that, Kalo got angry and raised his long staff up in the air.

"You see this staff? Well, I'll give their little behinds a good beating with it!" he declared menacingly.

Chapter 4

The Iron Trap

The town of Y, which sits on the banks of a river originating at Lake Kegham,[*] is one of those towns that still haven't shaken off the dust of their Persian past. Here even the Armenian is a Turk, the Turk is yet more Turkish, the women dye their hair with henna, and the men wear narrow trousers together with Persian slippers.

Brother Aved had spent the whole day selling his produce in the marketplace. When evening came he went and stationed himself in front of a certain rich man's store, his head bowed and leaning on his long staff. He glanced uneasily at the store from time to time, hesitant to approach; a stance in which he cut the figure of a man condemned and waiting for his sentence to be read.

He stood there for a long time waiting to be noticed and called inside, and standing beside him, equally mute and still, was the Easter lamb he had brought to town for the agha. Like its master who stood there in the grip of tremendous anxiety, the lamb seemed to have lost its natural vivacity. Little Kalo sat on the ground holding onto the lamb's feet so that it wouldn't run off. He was the only one of the three who didn't have a care in the world as he looked around at everything that was so new and exciting to him

"Does the agha have any little boys, Uncle?"

"No, he doesn't," Aved answered gently.

"Then who's going to play with the lamb?"

Aved didn't answer. Just then he heard someone call to him:

"Ah, so it's you Brother Aved."

At this Brother Aved seemed to wake up from a reverie. He looked up to see one of the young men who worked for the agha. He drew back humbly and bowed his head to him.

"You must have come to see the agha," said the young man.

"How could I leave without seeing him?"

"Did you bring any. . . you know. . . ?" the young man asked, rubbing his thumb and forefinger together.

Aved nodded in the affirmative.

The young man disappeared into the store and several moments later Aved was called to the door. The two victims, Aved and Kalo, stood there awaiting their fate. . .

Brother Aved entered with a great deal of trepidation and bowed deeply toward a squat, white-haired man sitting across the room perusing a stack of letters at a table.

His submissive gesture went unnoticed. He scratched the nape of his neck and coughed a couple of times to get the agha's attention. When the agha finally looked up and noticed him, Brother Aved paid his respects with yet another deep bow.

The agha was particularly courteous to people who had accounts to settle with him, and in these cases his obsequiousness descended to the coarsest hypocrisy. Seeing the peasant standing before him an uncharacteristic smile flashed across his coarse face.

"Hello Brother Aved, how are you? How are your children and family? Well, I hope," the agha said, greeting him.

"We're getting along well enough, but may the Lord cut short our years and add them to yours," said Brother Aved.

"Are your animals and crops doing well?"

"The animals aren't doing badly, thank God, but may He have mercy on me, my crops have dried up and they're just sitting there. There hasn't been enough water because the rain never came. We went to the priest. He looked in the scriptures and told us the heavens had been sealed up."

The agha now saw an opportunity to take advantage of the peasant's superstition:

"That's why I urged you to come and pay your debts on time, but you didn't listen. Don't you understand? It makes God angry when you act like that. Trade means trade, don't you see? I give you something and you give me something back. It doesn't mean you just take what I give you and eat it up. I'm not really talking about you, Brother Aved. You're a good man like your late father was, but I'm talking about people like that no-good Kevon Tatosyan. He disappeared with my twenty manets a year ago and I never saw him again."

"He's just a poor fellow with a family to support. You've got to give him a break. How can he help it if he doesn't have the money? When he has it he'll pay you back and redeem his honor," said Brother Aved compassionately.

"But what about me! I'm poor and have a family to support, too," said the agha angrily.

"God's been good to you, agha, and may He bless you with even more, but Kevon is completely broke now."

"No, Brother Aved. You're a sensible man but you still don't understand," said the agha, gently admonishing his guest. "If I just let everyone get away with that, then I'll end up like you."

"True, agha, but you should still give people a little break. Do the villagers eat the money up? No. When they get some, they pay it back. You're the master here below and God rules above, but we go without food and drink and send our children to bed hungry just to come and pay off our debts to you."

The agha began shuffling through his papers again to find Aved's debt.

He handed the piece of paper to his assistant, saying, "I know that Brother Aved brought the money with him. Take a look at his account."

Brother Aved could see that his interview with the agha was over. He approached the agha's assistant, reached into his breast pocket and pulled out a handful of money and handed it to the man without counting it out.

Turning Brother Aved over to his assistant was a deliberate tactic on the agha's part, comparable to a hunter dangling some bloody prey in front of his dog's nose to excite his instincts. The assistant's eyes went back and forth between the wad of money, which he turned over to look at on both sides, and the account. "It's still fifty roubles short," he said finally.

Brother Aved was completely stunned. "But I only owed fifty at most. How could it not be enough?" he said in desperation.

"Ah well, you didn't figure in the interest. What you gave me barely covers it," the assistant said brusquely.

"Brother Aved, no one's asking you for more than is due. Why get so upset, son?" said the agha from across the room. "Give him some of the interest money back, Krikor. He's a good man and he'll appreciate it. Give him a little something from your pocket, too. It'll be for his children.

After all, it's Easter and they deserve to be happy."

Slyly tacking on more debt, then handing out little gifts to peasants was one of the agha's tried and true business tricks. Thus, Brother Aved was handed a couple of colorful handkerchiefs and a length of plain cloth. He took them and blessed the agha's life.

The assistant drew up a new debt note and presented it to Aved with instructions to dip his finger in ink and press it on the paper as a seal. Brother Aved was quite familiar with this procedure and did as he was told.

By this time Kalo had become quite bored with waiting alone outside and from time to time poked his head inside the door, took a few looks, then finally withdrew so as not to be noticed. Having concluded his business with the agha, Brother Aved suddenly remembered the lamb he had brought for him and called for Kalo to bring it in.

"So you brought me an Easter lamb, long life to you!" the agha said.

Kalo blushed with embarrassment and beads of sweat started rolling down his forehead. Never in his life had he drawn the attention of such an important man.

"How old is the boy?" asked the agha.

"He just turned twelve," answered Brother Aved.

"One might take him for fifteen. What is it the peasants say, he ate more than his due and got big doing it?"

The agha had a specific reason for being interested in Kalo. His wife had been saying for a long time that he should find a peasant boy to be a domestic servant in their home. She felt that the boys in town were too naughty to be relied upon for such a job. They stole everything, yet it was impossible to catch them at it or get back what they had stolen, whereas a peasant boy would be innocent and docile. This was why the agha now contemplated taking Kalo away from his uncle.

"You know what, Brother Aved?" said the agha in an entirely normal tone of voice. "Your late brother was a very good man, and may God shed light on his soul. You're a good man, too, but he was special, and I'd like to do him a good turn for the sake of my soul. Do you know what I mean? I'd like to take his son and raise him to be a real man. Do you understand? A man – a man like me, not some ignorant peasant. . ."

The word "man" in the agha's parlance had a special meaning. He meant a wealthy entrepreneur, since to his mind anyone who didn't have money couldn't be regarded a real man.

On hearing what the agha had just said, Brother Aved was thrown into great anguish and stood there for many moments at a loss to answer. He finally spoke up in confusion:

"I don't know what to say, agha. You know best. You understand things so much better than us."

"God bless you, son, well said," the agha answered gravely. "You're a sensible man, and you wouldn't let your brother's son fall into misfortune. And something else – if you give us the boy, you can eat and drink as much as you want with us and our door will always be open to you."

Kalo barely paid any attention to this discussion that would seal his fate. His attention was rather drawn to the various articles in the store, particularly a fascinating little cardboard horse sitting on a narrow shelf.

"What a cute little horse," said Kalo to a young apprentice boy standing near him. "What does he eat?" he asked. The boy smiled at Kalo's simplicity and advised him to be quiet so as not to embarrass himself.

"So, do you understand now?" the agha went on, addressing himself to Brother Aved. "You'll leave the boy with us. I'll feed him and clothe him like my own son, and when he gets older and understands things I'll pay him a monthly salary."

In a certain way Brother Aved felt happy that his brother's son would enjoy good fortune and some day turn into a "man", to use the agha's word. On the other hand, he thought of the fact that he would at the same time lose a very valuable asset, for Kalo was quite useful to him. But to mention such a practical reservation would have been out of the question, since he was in debt to the agha and "the debtor should be shamefaced and keep his words to a minimum."

Certain terms were agreed to – or more accurately, not agreed to – except for the agha's promise to feed and clothe Kalo. As time went on and Kalo became capable of doing "regular work" he was supposed to begin receiving a monthly salary, but all real specifics were deferred to the future, and no one ever bothered to ask Kalo how he felt about it all. When his uncle informed him of the arrangement that had been made, Kalo's response was, "I won't stay here."

Brother Aved gently tried to convince him, saying that the town was better than the village, that he would come and visit him often, and other such things, but it was useless and Kalo wouldn't agree.

"I won't stay here," he repeated. "I'm going back with you."

But then Brother Aved became more forceful, and the poor boy's eyes filled with tears. It was with these tears that his new and melancholy future would begin, and he was almost taken by force from his uncle and delivered to the agha's house.

Brother Aved left town very sad, wondering how he could break the news to his old mother and what he could do to console her, knowing that she could hardly go on living without the hope of someday seeing Kalo again.

"You took the boy and lost him," was all she could say on hearing Brother Aved's story when he returned.

Chapter 5

The Golden Rooster's Realm

In one of the back streets of the town of Y sat a one story house distinguished by its dilapidated walls from all the others around it, its low door and narrow windows suggesting a prison. Though the neighboring houses had changed in style over time, this house remained just as it had been before the advent of European architecture and retained its immemorial Persian style. A narrow gate opened into a large yard shaded by ancient mulberry trees. These had assumed grotesque forms after long ago losing their bark and being exposed to decay. There were also a number of walnut trees, old willows and half dead apricot trees scattered here and there among them. Grapevines had grown up their desiccated trunks and filled their barren branches with a verdant mass of foliage. Though a home stood nearby, the trees showed no sign of human care.

There were also a number of run-down shacks here and there, again in no particular order. They had collapsed almost to ground level beneath the ravages of time, and with their dusky, mournful shapes completed the dreary atmosphere of a setting that resembled the haunts of one of those legendary spirits who hated newness and with self-indulgent obstinacy clung to ruin and decay. This dreary place was home to the richest man in town, Bedros Masisian – or "the agha" as everyone called him.

Masisian didn't neglect his property out of miserliness, but rather out of a superstitious belief that had become central to his life, namely, the belief that a house exercised a mystical influence over its inhabitants and that the good or bad fortune of those who lived in it was tied to certain supernatural qualities belonging to the house itself. According to this belief, there are houses in which children die, the owners' lives are cut short and poverty is always written on the walls. Even a rich man who moves into one of them will soon fall into poverty. On the other hand there are houses – Masisian's among them – that have a beneficent influence on people's lives. The good luck of such houses is connected with some invisible creature that lives in it, often a snake with a jewelled crown, but in Masisian's case it was a 'golden rooster'. According to the tradition handed down in his family from generation to generation, the 'golden rooster' together with his 'golden hen' and chicks had many times appeared to his forebears.

The golden rooster had disappeared in Masisian's father's time, whereupon his good fortune "went to sleep" and he fell into poverty. But in Masisian's day its effects began to manifest themselves again, his hearth was blessed once more with good fortune, and his house came into its own once again. For this reason every bit of worn brick or decaying wood had a particular meaning and had to be kept just as it was lest the magic spell be broken.

Masisian wasn't one of those men whom we in Persian call a 'novkisa', which is to say a nouveau riche. The nouveaux riches are quite different from those who have inherited their wealth, for they myopically see no worth or power in anything but money. They mistakenly believe that simply because they have a lot of money, which they ostentatiously call attention to, they thereby also have fine minds and character and honor. But, in fact, these men are nothing but anomalous individuals who try to cover their peculiarity with a mask of gold.

No, Masisian didn't belong to their number. On the contrary, he never boasted of his wealth or put on airs. He was rather quite modest and tried as much as possible to avoid calling attention to what he had.

His view of money was different. For instance, he would say that no one brags about having two eyes, two ears, two hands, etc., because this is the most natural thing in the world. By the same token, one shouldn't flaunt one's money, since it's a basic necessity without which a person is seriously hampered in life.

But on the matter of making and accumulating money – the 'golden rooster' aside – Masisian felt that the entire world was 'there for the taking' and that if you didn't want to starve to death you'd better get as much as you could out of it. As for the methods chosen to do so, that wasn't important as long as they did the job. And thus, because he acted quite naturally and without premeditation or malice, his conscience was always clear.

Masisian's father had been a butcher and in his youth he had helped him in his trade. Butchers and executioners have a great deal in common: one executes animals, the other people. This is where Masisian acquired his severity, a trait that often assumed quite barbarous forms. But these severities were confined to his home and family, for he was the type of man of whom it is said, "The devil in his house and a lamb outside." His solicitousness toward others often descended to the most vulgar forms of ingratiation. Possessing the elasticity and suppleness of a serpent, he took whatever shape was necessary – and had a serpent's venom in his fangs, as well.

It was never his intention to present a false image. On the contrary, he saw nothing wrong with the way he did business, for he firmly believed that this was the only way he could survive. He summed up his outlook with the sayings, "If you find yourself in a town with one-eyed people, then take one eye out so that you fit in," and "A brittle vase is soon broken." In other words, it was necessary to be soft and flexible and bend whichever way or take whatever form circumstances required to remain in one piece. There was no dishonesty in this thinking. Everything he did sprang from clear conviction. He followed whatever life demanded of him, and if that required taking crooked paths then the blame shouldn't be placed on him but on the forces that had pushed him in that direction.

Masisian's career began when he broke with his father's trade and started buying horned animals from the country to bring to town and sell to butchers there. This is a type of slave trade. Anyone acquainted with this trade, the selling of animals, will agree that the character of those who engage in it is not very different from those who conduct a similar shameful commerce in Africa.

As Masisian got richer he expanded his business into other areas, and with the help of his 'golden rooster' one day became the richest man in the province.

But successful men with lowly origins often make a great effort to deny their families' true history and portray themselves as more refined than they actually are. Masisian started out without such grand pretensions but eventually succumbed to them out of a simple desire to establish a respectable name for his family. This could be done quite easily by looking for a name in the annals of Armenian history. He picked the name Masis because all the other names were taken.

It's nothing new for Armenians to steal the names of illustrious ancestors while falling far short of their virtues. We have among us these days many Arshagunis, Bagratunis, Mamigonians, Amadunis, Pahlavounis, Gamsaragans, not to mention all the names of famous mountains, plains, and rivers that have become the family names of lower class people, so much so that if the great Armenian historians were to come back they'd think that all the famous families of the past had been resurrected and were going on with their lives.

Chapter 6

Holy Thursday

Masisian had a small family, just two daughters and a son remaining at home. His first child, a daughter, had hanged herself in the woodshed for reasons that won't be told out of respect for the poor girl's memory. . . The next oldest child, Nuné, had waited and waited for her father's permission to marry, but seeing that he would never give it she at last ran off with one of his employees and married him and settled down to live in his native village. At first Masisian cursed her, but as time went on he put her out of his mind and never mentioned her name again, as if to do so would sully his lips. On those few occasions when he was reminded of her, he insultingly referred to her as "that tramp." From the day she left she was banned from home, only returning as circumstances allowed to secretly visit her beloved mother. Masisian's son Stepan had finished his studies at the gymnasium,* but his father had prevented his going on to university on the grounds that this would ultimately only spoil him. So Stepan was forced to come back and live at home. For years he went about town wearing his gymnasium uniform, all the while pestering his father about returning to school to complete his studies. His father turned a deaf ear to his pleas and forced him to work in the family business, a situation that fostered endless misunderstandings and conflicts between the two.

The two daughters who remained at home were ten year old Gayané and seven year old Hripsimé. With these two girls it seemed that nature had chosen to prove the breadth of its taste, making an exemplary beauty of one and quite the contrary of the other – and their personalities were just as different. The less pretty of the two,

Gayané, was altogether timid and kind, whereas the pretty one, Hripsimé, was arrogant and naughty. To round out Gayané's homeliness, she was lame in both feet and rocked from side to side when she walked. People with abnormalities of the body are usually talkative, sarcastic, abusive. She showed some of these traits, as well, in addition to her kindliness.

Their mother's name was Mariam. Now it sometimes happens that luck, fate, providence – call it what you will – plays remarkable tricks in the pairing of a couple. You'll see a pretty woman with an ugly husband, and vice versa; an intelligent woman with a dull witted man, or vice versa; a short husband with a tall wife, and a tall husband with a short wife. In the pairing of spouses nature seems to have no rules, and this was the situation Ms. Mariam found herself in. She was as kind and considerate as her husband was harsh and severe. In this Gayané was like her mother, while Hripsimé was more like her father.

And so it was into such a household that Kalo – that joyous, carefree little peasant lad – had fallen. It was to this household that his fate was tied, and this will be the subject of our story.

Until Kalo arrived the Masisian home had got by without a servant. Especially after one of Masisian's daughters had run off with one of his employees, men were always kept away from the house. Masisian himself would buy whatever the family needed in town – meat, vegetables, fruit, etc. – and bring it home wrapped in his handkerchief. If he chose to send one of his helpers home with something from town, he was only to leave it at the door and return immediately to work. Masisian strictly enforced this regime and thus kept his home entirely free of men.

But even in Persian harems young boys between twelve and fifteen years old are allowed to be servants, and that was Kalo's age.

He joined the household for the first time on Maundy Thursday, and the arrival of this exotic little peasant boy touched off a flurry of laughter there.

"So. . . . this is the new servant you've found for us?" Mrs. Masisian said mockingly to her husband, looking the boy up and down as he stood there in confusion.

"Well, what do you think? I picked well, didn't I?" said Masisian with self-satisfaction. "He'll be as good as ten men. Look at his hands and feet. You'd think he was an ox just brought out from winter rest!"*

This comment didn't sit well with Kalo. "I'm no ox. . ." he piped up in defense of his own dignity.

The couple looked at him sharply but said nothing. Instead, they invited him into the cookhouse for something to eat.

"He's got a sharp tongue, it seems. He was raised with no manners at all, and he's never got a good whack from a teacher, but he'll be a good worker," said Masisian.

"Maybe and maybe not. Let's just hope he doesn't steal," responded Mrs. Masisian.

"Not now, at least. He's too young for that. Later on when he's learned a thing or two, that's when he'll start to steal," said Masisian.

"I won't let him learn that," said Mrs. Masisian.

"You can try, but how can you keep him from learning it?" said Masisian, wagging his head as he laughed. "There's a lot of things we don't allow, but people learn them anyway without being taught. You can't keep a newborn gosling from jumping into the river. As soon as it's out of the egg it heads for the water. Where did it get that, and who taught it to swim?"

This conversation took place in the garden as husband and wife sat beneath a willow on a bench covered with a blanket. Stepan, their son, sat in the garden not far away, studying an insect with a magnifying glass. On hearing what his father had just said, he broke in on the conversation:

"A gosling runs to the water out of instinct, but there's no such thing as a stealing instinct in people. That's something learned from bad example. It's due to a lack of proper training and the other conditions of life."

To be sure, Masisian had no comprehension of what his son was talking about. "Be quiet, you don't know what you're talking about," he said with a frown.

Chapter 7

Mikayel

Although in the beginning Kalo found losing the freedom of village life and his separation from his dear friends and cherished sheep very difficult, this half-wild "bear cub," as Masisian had referred to him on first sight, gradually adjusted to his new circumstances. The reader will recall that Kalo first joined the household during Holy Week. Quite naturally, even family dogs and cats fare better during such holidays. Thus, despite their usual frugality, the Masisians were quite generous with him during these days. At first every little thing he did made them laugh, and they treated him as a mere curiosity. Eventually they sought to train and refine him, a task in which Mrs. Masisian took primary responsibility.

Within a few days Kalo was hard to recognise – at least from outer appearances. Instead of his large hide cap, he was given Stepan's gymnasium cap to wear. His peasant sandals were replaced with some of Masisian's old low-cut shoes which were too large for him and made walking difficult. He was also given one of Masisian's old cotton cloaks to wear over his tunic. This also was far too big for him and was bound at the waist with a black cord. It hung down to his ankles just clear of the floor and the poor child was lost deep inside this sack-shaped Persian garment.

In a word, Kalo was transformed from head to foot. And they even gave him a new name. In place of his peasant nickname, Kalo, they now called him Mikayel. But underneath it all he was still the same Kalo with all his country roughness, a roughness like that of a stone which in the hands of a skillful artisan can be given a beautiful lustre.

Kalo's days of happiness came to an end with the end of Holy Week. Despite Masisian's promise to give him a job in the store and train him in the business – in order to "make a man out of him" – the promise went unfulfilled and he was kept in the house as a domestic servant from the very first day.

Kalo was very clumsy in performing his assigned tasks. No sooner did he pick something up than it would fall from his hands and break. He was constantly losing control of small objects and they'd just go flying out of his hands. He couldn't even serve a cup of tea without spilling some. But a jug full of water he could easily deliver wherever they wanted it. He had no head for little objects, for it seemed he was made for greater things.

This boy Mikayel, as we shall henceforth call him, had to pay a high price for these little mistakes. If he spilled something he could expect to go hungry for the rest of the day, and everyone from the agha on down would harshly reprimand him, calling him "bear cub" or "peasant jackass", and so on, and hardly a day went by without such insults. But little Mikayel did have one defender in the home, Ms. Mariam. She forgave him as an innocent child and told her children not to report his little mistakes to their father so that he wouldn't be beaten.

As we know, Mikayel used to have a fine voice and sang beautifully in his native village. But now, having unfortunately fallen into an iron trap, the happy little bird fell silent and sometimes became so despondent that he tried to run away and go back to his village to see his dear pals and grandma again. But Ms. Mariam would have him caught on the way and brought back, whereupon she'd comfort him and convince him to stay once more.

Though she sometimes laughed at him, too, Gayané was generally kind to Mikayel and even set aside some of her dessert for him on occasion. But proud and beautiful Hripsimé couldn't stand the peasant boy and often complained about him to her mother.

Masisian's son, Stepan, loved Mikayel like his own brother. He bought a reading primer for him and tutored him when he had the time. But one day his father noticed what was going on and grabbed the book out of Mikayel's hands and threw it down.

"Do you want to spoil him so he'll end up like you!" he said to Stepan.

One of the few bright spots in Mikayel's new life was going to the marketplace where he might see some of his fellow villagers who had come to town to sell their produce. One such day as he was walking through the marketplace he caught sight of one of his old village pals.

"Hey Doun, Doun!" Mikayel cried as he ran after the boy. When he caught up with him he threw his arms around him and kissed him.

"I swear I didn't recognize you. What have you turned into, you look so dainty and all?" asked Doun.

"What can I do, Douny *jan,** that's the way they dress you here in the town. They changed my name, too. . . It isn't Kalo anymore. But tell me, Douny, have you been to my house lately? How's my granny and the little kids? What are they up to? Is Gyedj grown up yet? And Babi must be walking by now. . ." (these latter were his uncle's children).

Then without waiting for Doun to answer he changed the subject:

"What've you been doing, Douny? I'll bet you've been going for a swim at the river every day. Here they won' let you go near the water. The harvest must be about ready by now, isn't it? Who picked our apples? I just came to town to buy some vegetables and bread. My mistress told me it was time for me to start learning something about buying and selling."

Now Kalo changed the subject once more:

"Are our plums ripe yet? Have you seen our dog? Who takes our sheep out to pasture now? I don't like it here, Douny *jan.* My heart's broken and I just don't know what to do about it. But tell my granny you saw me. Who came to town with you? When are you leaving? It's really bad here, Douny *jan.* . ."

All of Mikayel's disjointed questions left his friend totally confused and he didn't quite know what to say.

"I came with my father to sell cheese. We're going back to the village today," Doun said at last.

"But have you had anything to eat yet? Here, have some bread. The butter in it is from town. My mistress gave it to me this morning, but I didn't eat it. It's a good thing, too, because now you can have it."

So saying, Mikayel took a piece of flatbread out of his pocket and handed it to his friend. The boy stuffed the large piece of fragrant bread into his mouth.

"What good bread this is! Do you have this to eat every day, Kalo?" he said in a half-stifled voice.

"Oh no! My mistress gave it to me on the sly so the agha wouldn't know. I'd be lucky to get crackers to eat every day, but I don't even get that."

Mikayel's eyes welled with tears on saying this, but he covered it up.

"When are you coming back to the village Kalo? The melons are ripe, and I've been eating and eating them and my father doesn't even say a word. I'll keep some for you."

"They won't let me come back, Douny *jan*," Mikayel answered sadly. "I really want to go back and see my granny and live at home, but they won't let me. They say to me, 'Are you still thinking about your little valley, bear cub?' Well how could I forget, Douny *jan*? What is there for me here? Nothing but houses and more houses. . . The people here take villagers for jackasses. . . As soon as you open your mouth to say something, they beat you up. . ."

Doun was a couple of years older than Mikayel, and on hearing his sad story he felt sorry for him.

"Come on, I'll take you back to the village," he said protectively.

"But how can I go? My uncle will slap me and ask me why I came back as soon as he sees me. No, Douny *jan*, I might as well just throw myself into the river and go under. . ." he said, his voice breaking with emotion.

Doun tried to make him feel better by promising that he'd let his uncle know how badly he wanted to come back. This cheered Mikayel up, and he wanted in some way to show his gratitude to his friend:

"You know, Douny *jan*, I just remembered that I left my knucklebones* buried under the barn door in a jug. Go dig them up. There's more than a hundred of them. Take as many as you want and divide the rest up with the other kids. I can't play with them anyway."

"But I won't give any to Tomas. He's a bad kid. I just got in a fight with him the other day."

"Give him some, too. He's our friend, make up with him," said Mikayel. "Friends have fights and then they make up. Last night I had a fight with Boghos, too. I hit him in the head with a stick and it drew blood."

"A fight with Boghos? What was he doing here last night?" asked Doun with amazement.

"It was in a dream, Douny *jan,* and as soon as I woke up I cried and cried about cracking him on the head. Tell me the truth Douny, is he all right?"

"He's fine. We were together day before yesterday. We went and ate apricots in his orchard."

Their conversation was interrupted by Douny's father who appeared and called to his son, "Who's that you're talking to? Come on, we have to go."

"Douny *jan,*" said Mikayel, grabbing hold of his friend's shirt as he was about to leave. "Now that you're leaving, please say hello to my granny and my uncle and everybody and let them know you saw Kalo."

"I will," said Doun as he walked away.

Mikayel stood for a long time looking after his departing friend, then suddenly realized how late it was and started running back to Masisian's house.

Chapter 8

The Best and the Worst

Three years went by, and in those three years there had been many changes in Mikayel's life.

Mikayel was no longer just a domestic servant but had by now become a trainee in the agha's store, a significant promotion in his status. But what had made it possible? Certain superstitions can exercise a powerful influence on men like Masisian. On acquiring a new horse or cat or dog in the home, their business sometimes takes a sudden turn for the better and they attribute the good fortune to the new animal, which thereafter they'll never part with. Such an animal becomes sacred to the home, and when at last it dies they'll bury its head under the main door of the house. This superstition can apply to certain people as well. It happens that on marrying a certain woman good luck comes to the home and she is cherished, but sometimes the opposite is the case and the woman falls into disfavor. The same can happen with newborn children. In this vein, someone who brings good luck to the home can come to be regarded as a kind of 'golden rooster'.

Leaving aside the merits of such beliefs, we can only say that from the day that Mikayel joined the Masisian household its fortunes began to improve unexpectedly. Masisian couldn't help but notice it and attributed it to the new member of the household, the little peasant boy. This was how Mikayel was introduced to Masisian's store.

But by this time Mikayel wasn't the same person he had been three years earlier. He had shed his peasant coarseness and was now a polished young man. Even his face had changed: the plump, rosy cheeks of a peasant child had now become smooth and fair. Only his fiery eyes remained as they had always been.

All the customers now acknowledged Mikayel, for he wasn't the sort of person to be overlooked. They all enjoyed talking with him and evincing a few witty remarks from him. He was always pleasant and helpful, and no sooner had a customer rolled a cigarette than Mikayel was ready with a light, or when a purchase was made, Mikayel would immediately wrap it up without being asked to and often carry it home for the customer.

But there were occasionally little disagreements between Mikayel and Masisian arising from their very different attitudes. For instance, a woman might come to the store to buy a length of cloth or a few pounds of tea. In such a situation, Masisian would typically launch into an entire story about what a good friend the woman's husband had been and how he felt obliged to give her the very best deal, etc. At this point he would turn to Mikayel and say, "Young man, please go and bring out the very best we have for her."

Mikayel would go and bring back the very best, but Masisian would frown harshly at his inexperienced apprentice and say:

"When are you going to learn about quality, stupid?"

"We don't have any better than that," Mikayel would answer innocently.

"What do you mean, we don't, you good-for-nothing?" Masisian would roar, then fetch whatever it was himself.

"But that's the worst we have," Mikayel would say when his master returned. But Masisian would act as if he didn't hear what Mikayel had said and would measure out or weigh the desired item and conclude the sale. Then when the customer was gone he'd turn to Mikayel and shout:

"You good-for-nothing! When will you ever learn and become a real man? When I tell you to bring the 'best', you have to get it through your thick skull that I mean the poor stuff. Is that clear?"

"I've never heard of such a thing! What about one's soul? Surely it would be lost," Mikayel would mutter to himself, setting the agha off on a long but futile tirade.

Chapter 9

Dirty Windows

Certain peculiarities of Masisian's store and his way of doing business call for closer scrutiny. His establishment was more like a large warehouse than a normal store, filled with all kinds of different things stored in utterly helter-skelter fashion. You could find almost anything here, from the most delicate toiletries and Muscovite confections to hunks of iron for blacksmiths and leather for shoemakers. There was kerosene, sugar, tea, toys, the local brandy, eggs and bulghur. Here a fine lady could find scented oils for her hair, and for the sick there was henna powder and menthol oil. Indeed, you might have found anything there. . . . but swallow's milk. The chaos of it all was famous throughout the province and had given rise to the local expression, "Masisian's store" to characterize any jumbled mess. Masisian was illiterate and anything having to do with reading was anathema to him. He kept nothing resembling a formal account of his business dealings, but *arevdur*[*] was a word he well knew the meaning of – that is, taking with one hand and giving with the other, and that was exactly the way he did business. He had no use for 'niceties' but rather kept all his accounts in his own head. He had a prodigious memory and knew every item in stock, how many he had sold, how many remained, how much he had to charge for each to make a profit, etc. He only put up with writing to keep track of debts owed to him by customers, something he was forced to do because of negative experiences with a few individuals. In these cases, too, he showed an incredible memory. Imagine a small box filled with hundreds of scraps of paper, IOU's all jumbled together and as mixed up as the contents of his store. Nevertheless, he clearly remembered whom each one belonged to, and when any of these debtors showed up in his store he'd find their IOU in the jumble, be able to tell them how long the debt had been owed, what the interest and the principal on it was, etc. Not only that, he could identify these aging scraps of paper after even ten years had passed and be able to declare how many kopecks each of them involved. He could also recall every detail of his life in complete detail, where and how it had occurred, the date, the hour, who was present at the time, the words exchanged, etc. Truth be told, his memory was practically supernatural. And if anything was missing from his store he would immediately notice it.

In addition, Masisian was rigorous and punctilious in his work. With the first chime of the clock in the morning he was dressed and ready to go. His first act of the day was invariably to go to church for morning services, which in this province take place very early. He always stayed to the very end of the service, then before the sun had risen went straight to the market square where Mikayel would have long been waiting for him with a basket on his arm. Masisian's first order of business would be to see what the peasants had brought to sell. He knew them all by name and even the names of their fathers, their sons, their wives. He'd go up to each of them, talk very nicely with them, ask how they were, and check the prices on their produce, even if he had no intention of making a purchase. The peasants always felt honored that such an important gentleman would take his time to talk to them.

But only the bear knows its own reasons for circling around the honeycomb with such delight – and it was enough for Masisian to find a gullible peasant who had some fish or fresh butter or poultry to sell. He would wear the man down with all sorts of banter, saying, for instance, that he and the man's father had been good friends, that he had helped his father out many times, and a thousand and one other such things, all to raise the man's hopes to the limit and drive him practically mad with expectation just to get what he wanted for a few kopecks less.

Masisian preferred to buy whatever groceries his family needed himself. "Someone else is only good at gathering thorns for you," he'd say. When he was finished looking around the market square he'd take his time going from fruit stores to butcher shops to bakeries, load Mikayel down with his purchases and send him off to deliver them home.

By the time Masisian arrived at his store his employees would already be lined up in front, ready to go to work. The first thing he did was to carefully examine the wax seal over the door locks, then hand the keys to one of his employees to unlock them. When they were unlocked he crossed himself, opened the door and went in. Mikayel would already have hurried home with the groceries for the day and returned to the store. Without losing a second, he would set about sweeping in front of the store and sprinkling water around, then he'd dust off the goods and help the other employees straighten them up. Being a typical Armenian merchant, Masisian saw to it that his goods were rearranged every day in order to give the impression of newness, and this was no small task for his workers. But one thing was fine just as it was and never touched – the dirt on the windows. "The dirtier the windows, the fresher the goods will look," he'd say.

Every morning, every day, this was how things were done without variation. Masisian was very finicky when he felt he had the right to demand something of others, yet he always made exceptions in his own case.

He stayed in his store from morning to night, whether in the biting chill of winter or the sweltering heat of summer, and nothing could move him from his spot. He was extremely suspicious of others – even of his own children – and regarded everyone but the peasants as thieves. In his view the peasants were reliable, but only because they were too stupid to be otherwise, for anyone with a hint of intelligence was prone to steal. So he kept a watchful eye over his store and didn't miss a thing that went on. When his employees had concluded a sale they would immediately bring him the money to put in his till. This till was very similar to the alms boxes commonly stationed on a post in front of churches or chapels, with only a thin slit in the top to put the money in and locks sealed in wax. He would open it and count the money only once a week, and that was on Saturday evening. This was also the only day of the week he'd pay anyone money. He followed certain mercantile superstitions and, for instance, you couldn't get a kopeck out of him on Monday because he believed that if he parted with any money that day he wouldn't make any the rest of the week.

But though, as we said, Masisian sat in place all day maintaining his Argus-eyed* watch over the store, sometimes nature would get the better of him despite his iron will, and – especially during the long, swelterings days of summer – he would start dozing where he sat. But then again it was really impossible to know if he was really asleep at any given time or not, because as soon as a customer came in and wasn't promptly served by one of his employees his eyes would instantly pop open and he'd shout, "You good-for-nothings, have you gone blind or what? Can't you see the customer's looking for something?"

But one event shook Masisian to the core and he had to admit that despite all his steely vigilance he had been violated and taken advantage of. This was around the time when one of his closest friends had just died. Masisian was always meticulous about religious observances and felt obliged to attend the funeral service. After the funeral he returned to the store all exhausted and found only Mikayel there, the other employees having gone out on various errands. He instructed Mikayel to keep an eye on the store while he went off to sit in his usual place. It was an extremely hot day.

The death of his good friend on the one hand and his fatigue on the other had combined to make him feel completely limp. It also has to be admitted that he had drunk one too many toasts in honor of the dearly departed. As a consequence, as soon as he settled into his seat he fell into a deep slumber.

Just then a very well dressed young man came into the store, looked around at the goods, then slowly approached the dozing proprietor. At the sound of his footsteps Masisian immediately opened his eyes.

"Please give me some money for this," said the young man, deftly slipping a gold watch out of his breast pocket and holding it up for Masisian to see. "Give me whatever you can for it, I really need the money. My wife is close to dying and I have to find her a doctor right away."

Masisian looked closely at the young man, then looked at the watch.

"It's not worth a bit more than fifty roubles," he said.

"I'll take it and God bless you, but you can take my word that I bought it in Moscow for eighty," said the young man in a hurried manner.

Masisian counted out the fifty roubles to him and the man left.

Mikayel had witnessed this entire transaction and looked on with special interest.

"That man was here just an hour ago looking at the watches. He went up and down and looked at all of them for quite a while, but he didn't pick one out. He said he was just checking the prices because he had one to sell."

"Well, he made off with my fifty roubles, didn't he!" Masisian roared.

"What do you mean, made off with them?" said Mikayel in amazement.

"I mean he pulled the wool over your eyes and got away with it!" said Masisian angrily. "That was our watch!"

"Nonsense! You think he stole it? Good Lord, can a well dressed, well mannered man like that be a thief?"

"Sure he can! It's a fine gentleman like that who steals, not a dummy like you!" Masisan roared. Then muttering to himself he said, "What a daring boy! God bless your mother's milk. The red devil himself couldn't have tricked me better than that. Ah, if you fell into my hands I'd give you a hundred manets just to stay and be my helper."

He then turned to Mikayel once more. "Do you get it, you good-for-nothing? That's what a boy with a bit of pluck can do," he declared. "He'll take an eyelash right out of your eye and you won't know what happened. Do you understand?"

Mikayel only stood speechless where he was.

Chapter 10

The Garden

Masisian's home, his ancient house, was just like his store. Just as in his store where every manner of decaying, cast-off object was offered for sale, in his home there reigned the same unwholesome, decadent, and stagnant atmosphere.

His house reminded one of an abandoned fortress long since deserted by its occupants and left to decay. Everything had been abandoned to the destructive forces of nature and fallen into neglect and disrepair. Only a few of the original outbuildings remained intact: the cookhouse for making meals, baking and storing fresh food; and a storage shed where jugs of wine, fruit preserves and various malted grains were kept. The main house was divided into three rooms one of which served as the agha's bedroom/parlor/office. Another room was for his wife and daughters, in effect the women's quarters, and the third room belonged to the agha's son Stepan. It was a one story house with a floor of packed clay, like those in peasant huts, and an earthen roof with plants growing out of it. The three rooms were in line with each other, each with a door opening into the garden but without doors between them. Most of the light inside came through the doors. The windows were covered by dark immovable grates called "bencheren", a glassless feature of Persian architecture. Only in the winter were these sealed over with layers of paper made from old papers that the agha had brought home with him from his business. While providing some protection from the elements, this measure made it still gloomier inside. The exterior was plastered with a mixture of mud and straw which gave the house a somber, pitiful look.

The interior walls were covered with gypsum plaster which had long ago lost its whiteness and turned dark. Here and there pieces had fallen out exposing the underlying unfired brick. The ceiling beams were totally uncovered and had taken on the color of coffee. There wasn't a bit of European furniture – not a chair, table or sofa – but simply a broad wooden bench* ringing the walls, covered with rugs, mats and pillows, and this is where the family would sit in the cross-legged position.

Everything else was in shambles and seemed to have been neglected for a century or more. The barn, once filled with animals in his father's day, was now caved in and its roof rested on the ground. It was in this pathetic setting that the richest and most well-known man of the province lived. This was the setting in which "the golden rooster" worked its wonders to make good fortune abound . . .

Yet there were certain signs of life in the quite extensive garden. The paths were overgrown with plants long ignored; and the trees, struggling to stay alive, seemed to say, "Fear not, we'll live on yet. We'll get along fine without further human care . . ."

The life that went on in the midst of this dreary and abandoned wasteland corresponded entirely with its setting. It went on with the same unrelieved monotony and emptiness as in the neglected ruins of its grounds. Days, months, years went by in the course of which innovations and new fashions took their place in the world. But the Masisian home remained as it had always been, with a life frozen in place and as dead as the desolation around it, for Masisian looked at his life no differently than at his buildings or his property. Whatever was old was sacred, and it would be left as it had always been. Just as he'd make no repairs on the weathered and battered door that his father had used to enter his house, so he'd make no variation in the way of life of his forebears.

Bedros Masisian's home was like a complex organism driven by one solitary force, himself. Whatever he did, everyone else had to do; whatever was on his mind had to be on everyone's mind; whatever was interesting to him had to be the subject of conversation.

Everyone had to eat what he liked, go to bed when he did and rise when he rose – and woe to any who held back!

Every morning he'd go to town and buy what he wanted to have for dinner and, with very few exceptions, send it home with precise instructions on how to prepare it. Despite the resentment this caused, if the head of the household wished to eat nothing but stew, or dolma,* or kufteh* for an entire week, it made no difference at all to him that his family might have lost their stomach for such fare. If anyone spoke up and complained, for instance, "Akh, what's with the same stew, the same onions every day? . . . We'll die if we have to eat any more of it!" his usual response would be, "Well why haven't I died, then?" He judged everything by the "I" standard.

In Masisian one saw the very image of a selfishness that had reached the most grotesque level imaginable, reinforced as it was by a coercive nature. He was, in short, the very stereotype of the selfish personality.

Masisian's household economy had maintained its conservative simplicity. Knives and forks were unknown at his table; in fact, he considered it a sin to cut bread with a knife. Solid food was taken with the hands. Only for soups were spoons used. Whether he was entertaining a guest or not, Masisian always ate apart from his family. But guests were almost always on hand and he was a generous host. "Eating together can iron out a lot of problems", he used to say, but the problem was, once again, that his guests had to eat what he liked to eat. The daily stew or kufteh of Masisian's home had become almost legendary. His son Stepan used to take his meals with his father after returning home from studying in Tiflis, but at a certain point he couldn't get along with him anymore and stopped having meals with him and started eating with his mother and sisters at their own table. This isolation of the women that stemmed from Asiatic influences was a blessing for this otherwise joyless household. It sometimes happened that Mrs. Masisian secretly made a meal that her husband had not called for, but in such cases when the truth came out there was hell to pay for it.

The fact that the monster was gone from the house all day can only be ascribed to God's express providence. In his absence the family was able to breathe freely and enjoy themselves a bit. This enjoyment being constrained within the four walls of the house, the garden was the most congenial place for them to spend their time. It contained an old pond that was always supplied with ample water. Large trees lined its banks and their highest branches met over it to form a lovely green canopy that preserved a marvelous coolness along its banks even during the fiercest heat of summer. After doing all their housework Ms. Mariam and her daughters would relax here during the midday break. Gayané and Hripsimé would sit on a carpet, chatting and laughing with each other while they did their sewing, or becoming bored with that they'd throw pieces of bread into the pond to attract the fish, something that any child loves to do. All the while their mother would look on happily as she hovered about. Stepan would join them, too, after spending one of his long days tutoring children in people's homes. In the hot climes of the East, as in the town of Y, the abundant waters and ample gardens of the home were a special comfort to a family that led a cloistered life and had no pleasures outside of it. Without their garden Masisian's family would have been stifled to death in their lightless, airless house.

For the greater part of three seasons – spring, summer, and autumn – this was practically where they lived, enjoying their proximity to nature with its trees, grass, flowers and birds. Here on the shady banks of the pond they took their meals and entertained their guests, and at night slept in specially made *kedirs.*[*]

Chapter 11

Stepan

It was an extremely hot day, and the July sun was beating down. Ms. Mariam had set out a meal at the edge of the pond and was waiting for Stepan to return home and join her. But the usual hour arrived and passed and then another and another, and he still hadn't returned. The girls grew impatient and ate their portion, then started playing. The poor woman couldn't bring a morsel of food to her lips as she continued waiting for her son to show up.

Stepan appeared at last, sad and taciturn as usual. He passed by without saying a word and lay down on the carpet. His mother was in the cookhouse getting his meal ready. Gayané and Hripsimé were sitting on the grass dressing up their 'ladies' with newly sewn clothing, because the next day would be Sunday, and the neighbor's girls had to have a 'ladies' wedding. This intensive activity his sisters were engaged in drew Stepan's attention.

"Hripsimé, come here," he said.

"What do you want? I'm busy," answered little Hripsimé.

"Come here and I'll tell you," said Stepan.

Hripsimé went to her brother and leaned over his chest.

"How can I play with you? You don't have a 'lady'" she said.

"Step on me or pull my hair or whatever you want, Hripsimé."

"Won't you spank me if I do?"

"No."

Little Hripsimé laughed and ran away.

There are those moments in life when one is upset and tries to dispel anger with childish distractions, and such was young Stepan's state of mind at this moment. He stretched out even longer on the carpet and looked up into the trees as if trying to hear in the rustle of their leaves some hint of what the future might bring. This frail, sad youth with his fine and graceful features seemed older than his eighteen years, a stormy age at which the fire of youth erupts with all its power. Not so with Stepan. On the contrary, he was so distant, so distracted, so taciturn that at first glance one could surmise that he was troubled by some inner, secret torment. Yet there were those moments, especially when in good company, that he could forget himself, be more talkative and animated than usual and manifest the full sparkle of youthful vigor.

He had done a lot of reading and soon fell in love with the world of ideas, the kinds of ideas that so often inflame youthful minds, ravish their imaginations and turn them into deluded individuals. Before having learned anything truly fundamental or pursuing any field of study to completion, such individuals set aside hard work and pursue the illusion that they'll accomplish something great in the world without first preparing themselves. This illusion hinders their development and turns them into a class of mediocre novices who, instead of recognizing their own limitations, fall to hating and railing against a social order that makes it impossible for them to achieve their lofty ideals because it doesn't appreciate or understand them.

But Stepan remained largely free from the infection of such ideas, because up to this point he hadn't dealt with society in general and therefore had little reason either to hate or love it. His experience had been with the family in which he had been raised and personally born the brunt of every kind of bitter abuse arising from its coercive order, and therefore the only hatred he bore was toward its suffocating tyranny. He wasn't aware yet that the family is just another link in the chain of the social order and that its negative characteristics extend to society at large.

Abasement can be endured and even become imperceptible to a person who has never known freedom. Oppression within the home becomes bearable and entirely natural to its subjugated and abused members, since they have no knowledge of anything better. Stepan couldn't have grasped the repression and perversity that had dominated his childhood from his earliest years at home, but on leaving home for the first time and going away to attend school his awareness began to develop. It was only then that he began to fully see how unhappy he had been, and the horrid reality of his past suddenly weighed down upon his heart. An experience like that constitutes a stunning revolution in one's life, like the experience of a drunkard who suddenly sobers up to see and feel the wounds on his body. Stepan's eyes suddenly opened with self-recognition as scene after scene of buried memories opened before him in a crowded, complex panorama, each one sadder and darker than the one before. It was at this moment that he conceived the bitter hatred and raging vengefulness of a man who realizes that he has been duped, that his innocence has been exploited, that he has been held down and deprived of what he most vitally needed and rightly deserved.

Stepan's hatred for his father's domination could only harden on seeing that his mother, who had always been good to him and loved him with all the heartfelt tenderness of motherhood, was even worse off than he and a pitiful victim of the same domination. He saw that his innocent and lovely sisters had never once heard a kind word or even received a smile from their father but, quite the contrary, had been confronted with a cold, crude severity. They had always feared their father as they would have a demon or a rabid wolf.

Stepan was still lying next to the pond looking up at the trees when his mother came out of the cookhouse and asked him if he wanted something to eat.

"I was just trying to fall asleep. I'm terribly tired," Stepan replied flatly.

"What's wrong? Aren't you feeling well? Your face looks completely different," his mother said, examining him closely as she sat down beside him.

"I'm not sick, just let me rest a while."

"Why don't you have a little something to eat?"

"I've already eaten," he answered. He explained that he had gone to see a friend off, a young man who was leaving home to attend university in St. Petersburg. He and some friends had put together a farewell picnic for him in a farm, and they all had a good time together eating and drinking, singing songs and playing a number of jolly games.

"But it doesn't make sense to be so sad after having so much fun," his mother observed with a kindly smile.

"Nevertheless, Mother, that's the way things are sometimes. My friend finished gymnasium one year after me and now he's already on his way to university to finish his studies, but I'm still stuck here."

This put an end to his mother's momentary cheer. "That's enough, son, don't dwell on such things. What you've learned up to now will do," she said, but Stepan didn't reply and just continued staring up at the trees and listening to the gentle rustle of the leaves.

His mother tried to comfort him, saying that higher learning was only necessary for bureaucrats and other such people, that its goal was just to earn some money and a crust of bread, but that – thank God – money was no problem for him, since his father was the richest man in town. So why did he have to leave home and hearth, his mother and sisters, cut himself off from everyone he knew to go off and torment himself with the conviction that he had to read all the books there were?

"Let up, Mother!" said Stepan crossly. "I can't get you to understand that you don't get an education just to become a bureaucrat or make money. You just don't understand that there are higher callings in life than that. As for all my father's wealth, I don't even want to hear about it!"

"But if it's not for you, then who for? You're his only son."

Stepan had never before spoken in anger to his mother, but her latest comment was too much for him. His face registered a thousand changes of expression, his lips trembled and his eyes reflected unspeakable turmoil.

"I spit on that wealth you're making such a great point of, Mother!" he said with intense bitterness. "I don't need it. There's a curse on it and it'll be cursed forever. It's disgusting! Every kopeck comes stained with the blood and tears of thousands of people."

He went on to explain that the reason he had stopped his gymnasium studies at the sixth form was because he didn't want to take his father's money any longer; that if it had taken him that long to arrive at his decision, it was only because he had been a child and didn't really understand what kind of man his father really was. At that point he decided to rely on himself and make money by giving fifty-kopeck tutoring lessons and he would continue doing it until he was able to return to his studies.

"Then you're still planning on leaving home!" his mother cried out pitifully.

"Yes, and soon most likely. If it weren't for loving you and wanting to be with my sisters, I would've been long gone from here."

His mother's eyes welled with tears. She told him that she didn't wish to stand in the way of his plans because he was the light of her eyes, but she pleaded with him not to walk out of her life and leave her alone and unable to see him every day. She poured out her heart and confessed that she was very, very unhappy; that she hadn't had one happy day in all her life and that in her heart she really only wished to die but for leaving her children alone, "because their father never gave them a thought." She said that she had placed all her hopes on Stepan, but being denied that hope would be an impossible blow for her to sustain.

Stepan was touched by the genuine sadness of his mother's words and could only tell her that he was sorry for causing her so much grief.

His mother added that there was no way to change his father, that he would always be the way he was, but that Stepan would do well to try arriving at some sort of reconciliation with him; for his father didn't bear him any ill will but loved him. He just didn't want it to show. She said that his father boasted about Stepan when he was with other people, though he kept this from Stepan because he didn't want him to know he thought well of him. All of that stemmed from his father's egotism, for he couldn't tolerate his son's resistance but rather demanded unconditional obedience from him. His boasting to others about Stepan was similar to the way he bragged about the quality of his merchandise to customers, even when he knew it wasn't the very best.

She confided to Stepan that this type of behavior on his father's part was very hard for her to take, but that there was nothing she could do except advise Stepan not to make matters worse by doing things he knew his father didn't like. One of these was tutoring children in the homes of families that were poorer than his own employees, something that really rubbed him the wrong way because he considered it very shameful and worried what people would say about it.

But there was one other thing about Stepan that particularly galled his father, the fact that he had taken a role in a play that had him "spouting nonsense" on stage, something that was a terrible disgrace to his family. Stepan was, after all, an agha's son and it behooved him to comport himself accordingly. He therefore shouldn't fall into conversation with just anyone or visit any home or say hello to everyone equally. He should remain gravely aloof so that people would have reason to comment what a fine son the agha had raised.

"That's rubbish!" Stepan replied. "As for my tutoring, I'm just doing it to earn enough money for my trip to Moscow. And the play I took part in, that was only to raise some money for the friend we just sent off."

At this his mother became upset all over again. "So you're really planning to leave us?" she asked, her eyes welling with tears.

"Definitely."

Chapter 12

Khoja

Bedros Masisian was a unique character, a holdover from those somber Armenian *khojas*[*] who played such a significant role in commerce during the period of Persian rule, men who were respected not for their uprightness and honesty but rather for being capitalists and knowing all the tricky ways to use capital. With the decline of Persian rule and its replacement by a new political order he remained unchanged and went on dressing just like those *khojas* of yore: the same long robe and gown, the same shalvar[*] made of blue silk, the same Persian slippers; and, in a similar vein, his head was always covered with a flat, four-cornered cap made of black Bokharan leather such as our village priests still wear today. Through all the seasons, summer or winter, his clothing remained the same. He owned but one set of clothes and these he wore continuously day after day until he couldn't wear them anymore; but as to when that point was reached it was impossible to tell, since no one had ever seen him wearing anything different.

Bedros Masisian was a man of medium stature, heavy set, with a rotund body and a bit of a pot belly sticking out. His head tilted back so far on his short neck that it seemed it might tumble off. With shrewd eyes ensconced beneath bushy eyebrows, his face had a quite brutish look. His hair was always closely cropped, and his clean shaven cheeks were as fleshy and loose as his belly. A general yellowish hue, like that of Mongolians, pervaded all his features, even his ears and the whites of his eyes.

One of the many enterprises that he engaged in was usury, and he was one of the best known usurers in the province. Despite the large amount of capital at his disposal, his distinction in this field was that he had never lost a single large sum of money to anyone, but rather small amounts ranging from five to a hundred roubles. He had special confidence in the peasants and had therefore made a high number of small, high interest loans to them. In so doing he protected himself from the damage that any single default could do. Trusting in the intrinsic honesty of the peasants, he referred to them as his "milk cows" and to the interest he charged them as his "milk."

When a peasant came to ask him for a loan Masisian would invariably start the interview by grilling him on every aspect of his personal life. He had to know the names of his father and mother and whether they were still alive or not; the names of any siblings or children and whether they lived together or separately; what kind of property the man owned and where; what occupations he had been engaged in; which of those occupations had been successful and which had failed; and, finally, what he intended to do with the loan. If, for instance, the man said that he wished to buy a buffalo with the loan, Masisian would launch into a thousand and one observations about buffaloes, explaining how to cure this or that sickness in the animal, what kind of buffalo was the best, etc. And evasive answers to his barrage of questions would never do in successfully getting a loan from him, for even the cleverest liar would be helpless before the onslaught of his inquisition.

One evening a man came to his house to ask for a loan to invest in the cotton trade, a man with tousled hair, deep creases in his face and worn but well preserved clothes – one of those unfortunates who have become the victims of their own excessive honesty. Men like this always end up being duped because they lack the necessary cunning and duplicity to operate in today's completely amoral marketplace. They constantly complain about their fate but never give up the hope that someday they'll strike it rich despite all the odds. They throw themselves into their enterprises with every means at their disposal but in the end find that fortune has slipped through their fingers.

The gentleman had chosen to call on Masisian at his home in the evening so that he'd be able to have a good talk with him, since that would have been impossible at the store during business hours. He could be assured of a polite reception, since Masisian was always courteous with people who came to ask him for money.

Masisian was alone in his room when the man arrived, sitting cross-legged on the wall-bench near a narrow window, trying to cool off from the stifling heat. Near him was a large bowl of ice water from which he would frequently take little sips. Masisian wasn't a tea drinker, and his family only drank tea secretly or when they had guests. He was sitting almost half-clothed on a piece of worn-out carpet. All he had on was a tunic with missing buttons, and his chest hairs were sticking out of his collar. He had taken off his shalvar and socks, and his feet were bare up to his ankles, but his heavy hide cap was still on his head, something that was habitual with old-fashioned men. He'd never take it off even when he went to church. The room was dark when the visitor entered, and he asked for a lamp to be lit.

Finding his host in a rather embarassing state, the visitor sought to cover it up by talking about the weather:

"The heat is really stifling. There isn't a bit of a breeze. You're smart to deal with it like this."

"Well, son (Masisian called everyone 'son' no matter what their age), we have to thank God. If it weren't for the summer heat we wouldn't appreciate the spring. If it weren't for the cold of winter, we wouldn't appreciate autumn. God has created it all, good and bad. He's made the day to counter the night, and one man he's made rich and the other poor. If it weren't for poverty, we wouldn't be able to appreciate money."

Any such pronoucements Masisian made always concluded on the subject of money. His guest was quite preoccupied, and on the mention of money stated why he had come. Masisian left off with his general remarks, and his face took on a cool and matter-of-fact demeanor.

"So you want to try your hand at the cotton trade, do you?" he said, addressing the man in the second person familiar, since he never used the formal with anyone.

The man said he knew quite a bit about the cotton trade, that at the time of the American war to free the slaves he had made a good amount of money, but that later he lost it and now wanted to try his luck again.

"Luck has nothing to do with it. It's a matter of brains," Masisian said with the acumen of a specialist. "Tell me, how are you planning to use the money I give you?"

The man answered that by virtue of his familiarity with the trade he could make a good profit out of it and that he knew most of the cotton producing villages in the province of E. He said that all these villages had their middlemen who took in all the cotton produced there and had it concentrated in their hands, and that it was an easy matter to buy large quantities from them and bring them to town to sell to big merchants. He would thus be the middleman between village and town and multiply his capital many times over in the course of a year.

"But you see, you haven't learned a thing at all," said Masisian, and he launched into all the reasons the man was wrong and had no grasp of the business. He asserted that it was impossible to make money by buying it from the village *charchis*[*] and selling it in town, because the charchis keep the best product for themselves and sell only the dregs to merchants like him. If someone really wanted to make money, then he had to go and buy his cotton directly from the farmer the way charchis do.

"I wouldn't want to deal with a bunch of uncouth peasants," said the man.

Masisian bristled at his statement:

"You may not be a simpleton, but you seem pretty foolish to me. Goodness! That 'uncouth peasant' is exactly the person you have to deal with. How are you going to make any money off that devil of a charchi?"

It must be pointed out that the word 'devil' in Masisian's way of speaking had an altogether different meaning than the conventional one. If a man weren't some sort of 'devil', then he must be useless in Masisian's book.

Masisian always carried on at great length in conversations of this kind. Though in most cases he had no intention at all of granting a loan, he left no stone unturned in conferring advice on the applicant. Now having a clear picture of the man's approach, he explained that he didn't usually lend cash for such enterprises, but rather lent out small commodities that the peasants needed, cheap cloth and such. If only one were smart enough and knew the peasants well, this way of doing business was much more profitable than investing large amounts in the cotton trade. Peasants never have cash in their pockets but rely on credit to take care of their needs. But that's not a problem and one shouldn't be afraid to give them what they want, because they put their honor on the line and will never try to cheat a man out his money. It must only be understood that when it comes time to pay their debt, they don't pay with cash but with their product, such as cotton or other produce. Now – depending on how smart (or 'devilish') a merchant is, it's up to him to set a high value on the cloth he lets the peasant have. That way, when it comes time for the peasant to pay him back he'll have to do so with a large amount of cotton. This allows the merchant to profit in two ways: from the cloth, which the peasant is forced to accept at the highest price for lack of cash in his pocket, and from the cotton, which has little value to the peasant's mind because it's just been planted or is still far from harvest. The peasant pre-commits his crop as payment for the debt, and the value of his labor can always be downgraded when he finds himself in desperate need of cash or provisions.

The visitor listened quietly to all of this, then finally observed, "The business practices you've just described are no different from those of the charchis."

"Of course, because that's how you make a profit. And I'll tell you one more thing: there's a lot of variation in how to weigh things and the kinds of counterweights you use; you have to know what you're doing. In the villages they don't have iron weights, just plain stones, so you have to carry your own with you; even a brick will do, but of course one that's heavier than the standard. The peasant never questions how accurate the counterweight might be. So, for instance, if your brick weighs one and a quarter pounds and you use it as a one-pound weight, then you'll make ten times the normal amount of cotton. Do you understand? If you really expect to make a profit, that's what you have to do."

"But that. . . But that. . ."

"What're you trying to say, that it's stealing? Is that what you're thinking? But how can it be stealing when all the cotton buyers do it? If you don't do it that way, you'll lose out and go bankrupt."

The man had no response and Masisian went on:

"The peasants are really honest. They have a nice saying, 'The buyer's view depends on the seller.' They always give a little more than they have to. What's wrong with taking advantage of it?"

"Of course, but. . ."

"But you shouldn't trick them, is that what you're trying to say?" said Masisian, interrupting him with a chuckle. "But that's the way things are done nowadays. Everyone does it. There's no other way to do business."

While Masisian was thus engaged in expounding the satanic secrets of commerce, there was deep silence next door in Mrs. Masisian's room. Little Gayané was very sick. The cough she had contracted a few years earlier was now beginning to show the first signs of tuberculosis. Her mother, sister, and brother were sitting around her bed. Though Masisian was well aware of her condition, he didn't go in to see her on returning home because he was expecting his guest.

"We can't let her go on like this," said Stepan to his mother.

"But what can we do?" she asked helplessly.

"We have to call a doctor."

"But you know how your father feels about that."

"Of course, but we can't just let her die like this because he doesn't want to pay a doctor."

"It's not the money. . ."

"What is it then?"

Mrs. Masisian didn't answer but lifted a handkerchief to her eyes and began crying.

"I'm going to go see father right now and tell him he absolutely has to call for a doctor," said Stepan, quite worked up.

"For the love of God, please don't," said his mother grabbing hold of his hand. "He can get mad at me, but I won't open my mouth. If you go, who knows what'll happen?"

So saying, Mrs. Masisian rose and went to see her husband. She told him how sick Gayané was and asked him to call for a doctor. Masisian flew into a rage.

"What good will a doctor do? If she's fated to be sick, then a thousand doctors won't do her any good. And if her hour hasn't arrived, then you could throw her down from the highest mountain and she'd live through it."

But Mrs. Masisian continued imploring him, saying that their daughter needed a doctor, that everyone called for a doctor when it was necessary and that everyone couldn't be wrong to do so. But he wasn't convinced. Even his guest advised that a doctor be called. But Masisian was unswayed and totally ignored the man's comment.

"If you think you need a doctor, then I'll be your doctor," he said to Mrs. Masisian. "Go cook up a few heads of onion, sprinkle some salt on them, and give them to Gayané to eat. Her lungs will clear up and she'll get rid of her cough. Don't you know that's what I do when I get a cough?"

"Her cough is different from yours," Mrs. Masisian answered.

"Are you trying to tell me, for goodness sake! How is it different? A cough is a cough. A cough never killed anyone. I've had my cough for twenty years. So why haven't I died?"

Once again, the emphasis on the 'I'. Once again, looking at his daughter's illness from his own selfish, egoistic point of view, because a cough had never done him any harm and eating onions had helped. So what right did anyone else have to contemplate another cure? Since he hadn't died from a cough, his daughter had no right to die.

Knowing how stubborn her husband was, Mrs. Masisian left him where he sat without wasting her breath any further. She learned that Stepan had already gone for a doctor. Now she became more worried about the row that would break out with her husband when the doctor showed up than about Gayané dying.

When his wife had left the room Masisian found himself at peace again and resumed his conversation with his guest as if nothing at all had happened.

"It's truly said that women have a lot of time but little sense. You can't teach them a thing."

His guest said nothing in response.

"She slipped in like a little devil and interrupted us. What were we talking about?" Masisian asked.

"You were talking about how to use a pound and a quarter counterweight as a one-pounder."

"Right! Now, let me explain something to you."

Masisian then began recounting how at one time he had traded in silk in Noukh, Gakh, and other towns all over Lezgistan.[*] He said the people there were so ignorant they had no comprehension of weights and measures. This was at the most productive stage of his career, a period in which he had made the bulk of his wealth. These peasants were stupider than sheep, but nowadays it's a different story and they're all as sharp as the devil! Silk in those days would sell for the same price as cotton does now. Since few of the peasants had scales of their own, he carried his own truly wonder-working scale with him through all the villages. This was basically a conventional scale with a horizontal wooden bar with two baskets suspended from it by leather cords. But there was a special trick to operating it. For example, it allowed four pounds of silk to balance out a two pound counterweight. The trick had to do with manipulating the tip of the vertical bar, the part that one holds the scale with. This part was adapted to the action of the horizontal bar in such a way that if it were tipped toward the basket with the counterweight the silk would register lighter than it was, and if it were tipped toward the opposite side the silk would register heavier. The scale was therefore totally under Masisian's control to use to his own advantage. Such a marvellous scale it was that he had been pestered over and over again by an Agouletsi[*] merchant to sell it. The man began with an offer of a hundred roubles and raised it to a thousand, but Masisian still refused to part with the scale. Even to that day he had kept it – and would keep it always – as a sacred object that had brought him so much good fortune. . .

Having finished the story of his magical scale, Masisian now launched into a review of the various counterweights used in those days, an era when there were no prescribed types but the weight of twenty silver manets of a rouble was commonly accepted as the standard. He stressed that he himself had always preferred to use the extra large coins left over from Catherine's* time and had realized his greatest profits with them. It was said then that Zoks* used their right foot as the counterweight. After declaring their right foot to weigh five pounds they'd place it on one end of the scale and really bear down. That's how the Zoks took ten pounds of silk to everyone else's five and got so rich. Ah, what ever happened to those days! Gone for good! Ah, if you had a bit on the ball you could make a killing. . . and if you didn't you went hungry.

To hear him talk you'd think Masisian regarded all of this as something quite normal, that is, an era when people were ignorant and could easily be duped.

His guest listened with an occasional nod of the head, but finally had his fill and stood up to leave.

"Take care," he said to his host.

"Jackass!" he heard Masisian mutter to himself as he was leaving the room.

"Jackass!" thought the man to himself as he stepped into the darkness of the street.

Chapter 13

A Bed and a Book

As the saying goes, 'Better to be a dog in a home than a child,' for the child is ordered around by everyone, given a thousand and one things to do by the lady of the house, the agha, the servants – all of them with one thing or another to demand.

Though working in the store was a significant improvement in his status, from the very first day of his apprenticeship there Mikayel's responsibilities began to multiply and become increasingly unbearable. The poor boy barely had a spare moment. He still had to serve in the household along with his duties at the store. In the house he was on his feet before dawn every morning when everyone else was still asleep. He had to heat the water in the samovar, clean everyone's shoes, sweep the yard, then, as if that weren't enough, go to the stream and draw water to sprinkle the yard with. Oh, what a terrible ordeal it was for him cleaning that yard every morning! The dust seemed to shower down from the decrepit, crumbling walls, while the ground itself wasn't lined with stones but was just earth that had been packed down beneath the family's feet.

Despite all these chores, Mikayel still found the time to withdraw to an isolated corner of the house with his school book and study in complete silence. He had a very strong interest in learning to read and seemed to know instinctively that some day it would come in handy, but he had to do it clandestinely, for Masisian hated anyone who read, especially since his son Stepan had returned home from gymnasium and he found him an adversary with whom he could never be reconciled.

Mikayel chose to do his studying at night after everyone else had gone to bed so that he wouldn't be disturbed. His room was the former wood closet, now used to store household junk. Here were stored old crocks that could no longer be used, rusty nails and scraps of iron, broken shovels and pruning shears, saws with worn-out teeth, broken water jugs and cooking pots, tattered old shoes and slippers, bits of rope, a cotton carding machine, and other such things, all wasting away in dust and decay.

This airless and lightless cell resembled a large chicken pen, with only a small opening serving as its entrance and requiring its small inhabitant to bend down when entering. Despite all that Mikayel was grateful for his room, for here he could at least be alone. The junk that filled the room barely allowed any free space for him, and he only found a tiny spot free where he could lay his mat on the damp floor to sleep at night. This was an uncomfortable straw mat, as rough as a file, and it was painful to sleep on. After taking off his clothes he bundled them up and used them as a pillow. His blanket was an old, worn-out fur coat of indeterminate style or origin that had belonged to the agha and still bore only a few vestiges of hair. It was on such a miserable bed that, due only to sheer exhaustion, Mikayel found a sound sleep.

Late one night a particularly deep, desolate silence reigned in the Masisian home. There was darkness everywhere, except in one spot: in Mikayel's cramped little cell. Someone was walking softly through the garden and on nearing Mikayel's room noticed a sliver of light that escaped through his door and lit up a spot on the ground. The visitor lowered his head and entered the room. He found Mikayel lying on his rough mat, his head resting on his hands. His eyes were open but he didn't stir and seemed unaware that someone had entered. He was in that state of self-forgetting when the mind has stopped working and a kind of deathly numbness reigns over one's limbs. His school book lay open nearby.

In his half-sleeping state Mikayel was calling out, "Hey. . . Hey. . . Drive the sheep that way. . . that way. . ."

"The poor kid, he still can't forget about his sheep," said the visitor to himself.

It was Stepan.

In keeping with an established pattern he had come to spend some time with Mikayel and help him in his studying. He looked all around to find some place to sit and finally settled down on the carding machine. Mikayel didn't stir, and Stepan pushed on him gently to wake him up.

"Hit me. . . Hit me. . . Kill me, if you want. . . I still won't tell you anything!" Mikayel cried out.

"The poor kid is really delirious. He's really in a bad state," said Stepan to himself. "It's me, Mikayel, wake up," he said.

Mikayel lifted his head from the pillow and sat up.

"Here you've gone to bed in this careless way again. I've warned you a thousand times that you'll get sick that way," said Stepan, very concerned that Mikayel hadn't properly covered himself up.

"Oh, if I could just get sick and die!" Mikayel murmured plaintively, then burst out sobbing.

"What happened? What's making you cry?" asked Stepan.

It was at this point that Mikayel told Stepan the whole story: The agha had taken him to the cellar that day and given him a barbarous beating with a stick, then left him locked up there all day. He said he was terrified, on top of it, that he'd be spending the whole night there, but one of the agha's senior employees intervened. He told the agha that Mikayel hadn't done anything wrong and that he'd gone much too far in beating him. Mikayel said that luckily he had lost consciousness during the beating and didn't feel all the blows. He showed Stepan the black and blue marks on his body.

"Outrageous!" cried Stepan. Completely disgusted after examining Mikayel's injuries, he asked Mikayel what he had been accused of to get such a terrible beating.

Mikayel explained that the agha had more than once given him orders to spy on everything the family did and keep him informed. He wanted to know what they ate, who visited them, where they went, whom Mrs. Masisian talked to, where Stepan went on his outings, etc. But he refused to play the role of a spy. He told the agha that he knew nothing, but when the agha sometimes received bits of information about his family from his other workers he'd get angry at

Mikayel and say, "You little brat, why are you trying to fool me?" On that particular day Mrs. Masisian had given Mikayel some money and sent him to the market to buy some pears, apples, and apricots because Yeprem Agha's wife was going to pay her a visit. One of the workers told Masisian about it, but Mikayel denied it and was beaten for it.

"But why did you deny it?" asked Stepan.

"Because I knew if I didn't the agha would come home and raise hell with my mistress. I felt like I'd rather be beaten than have him raise his voice at her."

"So you love her."

"Yes. She doesn't beat me, but he always does. . . I'm not staying here anymore. I'm going to run away and just disappear. I've had enough beatings!"

Stepan tried to calm Mikayel down and advised him against doing anything of the sort, though it was clear to him what a terrible state Mikayel was in and how cruel his father could be. But he tried to convince him that running away would do no good, that he would only be found and brought back again and treated even more cruelly than before. This had already happened several times, because Mikayel was a kind of chattel, a guarantee of the debt being paid back that his uncle owed the agha. His freedom could only be contemplated after his uncle was freed from this debt. Stepan thought that at the right time Mikayel would be in a position to help his uncle, but believed that careful planning was necessary as to what he would do on being freed from his servitude in the Masisian home, because he feared that Mikayel might simply return to his native village and fall into the life of a peasant, while Stepan was convinced that with a good education he could really make something of himself.

But the compassionate advice of his friend, no matter how fine the feelings underlying it, could have had but little effect on Mikayel, for all he felt was the pain of his bruises and his own powerlessness.

"No, I'm going to run away no matter what and disappear wherever I can," said Mikayel. "But I won't go back to my village again so that they just come and nab me and haul me back again. I'll find some place . . ."

Now Stepan was truly shocked by Mikayel's despair and, knowing how bold and undauntable he was, feared that he might really throw himself seriously into harm's way, but didn't know what to do. Each of them – one the son, the other the servant – knew the other's situation very well. But the son was more unfortunate than the servant, because, being better educated, he felt his bondage more acutely; whereas the servant boy's feelings were simply of the moment, and with the healing of his bruises would probably also be healed the wounds in his heart.

Stepan stayed for a long time to counsel and console this poor boy whom he greatly loved. He saw so much potential in him that he didn't want to see his talents waste away here in this unwholesome atmosphere where circumstances had placed him. He vigorously urged Mikayel to heed his advice and not run away, but rather stay on long enough to absorb everything he planned to teach him. That would be his only chance to become a real man someday, but it would take patience, long-suffering and, above all, hard work. He talked passionately and without pause, from time to time flicking back the abundant hair which fell down over his broad forehead, and the dim light of the oil lamp imparted a special loveliness to the fine lines of his pallid face.

He had done a lot of reading. His heart had been filled and his thinking guided by that highest of all ideals, social enlightenment; that is, to love, to serve, to help those who are in trouble, those who are hurt and harried and oppressed by crude exploitation. Having returned to his father's house, he had only found it repulsive and disgusting – a place where his mother's tears had never dried and his sisters were oppressed. He returned to see a father who had eclipsed his family's sense of well-being, who deprived them of every pleasure, who seemed to have turned his household into a veritable hell, as he had turned his business into a real den of thieves. The most striking fact in all of this was the contradiction of a father who felt entirely at home with thieves and hustlers looking at his own son, a young man of impeccable honesty, as a thief whom he wouldn't allow anywhere near his store. Though stealing and trickery weren't vices in his father's eyes, if Stepan used his father's money without making up for it many times over he was seen as a thief.

Stepan concluded his lecture to Mikayel with an earnest warning not to sleep on the floor any more because it would make him sick, and he promised to take him to the doctor the next day so that his injuries could be treated.

"No way!" whined Mikayel. "If the agha finds out, he'll raise a big ruckus like he did when the doctor came to see Gayané."

And, indeed, Mikayel had good reason to fear, for the agha had raised hell the morning after he found out that his family had sent for a doctor. Not only that, he also sent a man to warn the doctor not to dare enter his house again.

"That won't be a problem. I've arranged everything so that no one will know. But now we have to make a new bed for you," said Stepan.

So saying, Stepan surveyed the junk in the room to find something that might serve as a bed and at last found a couple of planks still connected to each other from an old door that had been stored there. He rested one end of the planks on the cotton carding machine and the other on a windowsill, and the new bed was made.

"So – from now on sleep on that," he said to Mikayel.

"But what if the agha sees it?" asked Mikayel anxiously. "He told me to keep my hands off things in here and not move them at all."

"Take it apart in the morning and put it back the way it was, then at night fix it the way I did. So now you know what to do. . . Good night."

And Stepan left.

Chapter 14

Vartavar

It was three years later. . . Mikayel had grown up and turned into quite a fine young man, yet his basic condition remained exactly the same. He was clearly one of Masisian's best employees and had worked for him nearly five years, whether in his house or store. When his uncle had turned him over to Masisian it was agreed he would be paid a wage, but he still hadn't received anything. This was because he was considered inept in many of his responsibilities. He could never get it through his skull what 'good' and 'bad' really meant. Merchants have a special way of speaking among themselves, their own argot.

It couldn't be denied that Mikayel was slow to catch on to the wily ways of merchants and their argot. For instance, he still didn't know how to handle the measuring stick in such a way that he got eleven measures of cloth out of a piece that had only ten, nor a host of other such tricks in using weights and measures. For that reason, he was constantly subjected to scoldings by Masisian: "Fool! You'll never become a real man. . ." Masisian would say to him. His problem wasn't an inability to do those things, or even do them better than the other employees. His problem was that he hated such practices and saw them as immoral. This young peasant, by nature pure and unspoiled, had the good fortune of linking up with a fine young man like Stepan, for under Stepan's guidance he was able to develop and acquire an even purer character. Thus, an enlightened son bested a benighted father in influencing the young servant boy.

Stepan now became a student in the medical school at Moscow University. Mikayel would never forget the sad night before Stepan's departure from home. He was losing a good friend, one who had many times consoled him in life's bitterest moments and inspired him with so many lofty ideas. He was sitting on his bed in his miserable cell waiting sleeplessly to see Stepan one more time and listen to what he would have to say. Stepan entered suddenly with a small box in his hands.

"Here, this is for you, Mikayel, they're books," he said. "You've learned so much up to now, you'll be able to read and understand them all. Read them, and keep on reading. . ."

Mikayel happily accepted this precious gift and from that day on hid the books away in his cell. Though there was much in them he didn't understand, he would often spend entire nights reading them.

Mikayel was the only worker in Masisian's store who didn't have a family. All the others had parents or relatives in town and lived with them.

Their only work was in the store, and they didn't have to be domestic servants in Masisian's home. That burden was only Mikayel's to bear, even though his status was now higher than that of a common domestic servant, and the chores he was expected to carry out were quite offensive to him.

Ms. Mariam had many times suggested to her husband that he release Mikayel from domestic service and replace him with another, but the matter had never been resolved and met with the agha's consistent opposition.

"I don't have free food to give him. It won't kill him to work here and at the store, too."

But that 'free food' weighed very heavily on Mikayel. Despite all the unbearable jobs that had been foisted on him over the past five years, he still hadn't received a kopeck for his work, nor even a new set of clothes. He still went about in hand-me-downs that Ms. Mariam repaired and altered for him. But Mikayel had by now managed to save a modest sum from the tips he received from customers at the store, around twenty roubles, and with that sum he had a suit of clothes tailored for himself. Masisian knew nothing about it, and

Mikayel hadn't worn it yet, but kept it hidden away to wear on Easter to visit his native village.

Masisian generally preferred seeing his employees poorly dressed. In his view clothing was only for covering one's nakedness, not for enjoyment. By remaining poorly dressed his employees could always be sure he'd think highly of them: "Now – that's a man who knows what money's worth!" he'd say.

Furthermore, being purely self-centered in his judgement of others he took a decidedly dim view of people who adopted new fashions and decked themselves out from head to foot, while he, a wealthy agha, no more changed his style of clothing than he changed his skin. His employees had come to know him well enough to obey his expectations in every respect. When they were out of town it was a different matter, though, and they put on their finest, lived lavishly, wore gold watches with gold chains, and rode in carriages. But when it came time to report back to Masisian they returned totally changed, wearing their same old clothes and submissive expressions on their faces. For Masisian, you could do what you wanted as long as he didn't know about it. Every phase of his life simply rolled on, one after the other, in accord with its own set of rules. Just as he had never changed his style of dress, he had likewise never changed the organization of his house, his family, or his way of doing business. He was the very image of stagnation. Individuals, peoples and, ultimately, even nations that readily change their manner of dress also make rapid changes in the forms of their public life.

That Mikayel had a new suit of clothes was known only to Ms. Mariam and her two daughters. These innocent young girls had changed considerably by now. Gayané had regained her health and wasn't coughing anymore. Although the passage of years hadn't been kind to her in her physical appearance, her inner nature had to the same degree been enriched by many fine qualities. Hripsimé, by contrast, had developed into an even prettier girl, yet remained as scornful and conceited as ever. She was the only one in the family who didn't like Mikayel and she still maintained a cool reserve toward this peasant 'bear cub'. She persisted in recounting embarassing stories from the early days of his joining the household when he was still fresh from the country. But what bothered her most about him was his silence in the face of all her mockery.

Love between a family daughter and a servant boy often begins with small jests. Mockery, hostility, and insults are signs given when it isn't possible simply to say, 'I love you', or 'I like you.' But Mikayel was old enough to recognize Hripsimé's little wiles, and when he remained impassive to them, she'd typically say to him, "Why act so proud? If you want I'll go bring you your sandals. I've kept them for you," and she'd go and get the sandals he wore when he first joined the household. She thus intended to remind him of his previous condition and break his pride.

It was the time of Vartavar.[*] Outside the children were running up and down and shouting in the streets as they doused each other with water. The neighborhood girls had gathered in someone's garden and were drawing lots and singing the *Jan-Gyouloum.*[*] Life sparkled joyously everywhere; everyone was in the holiday spirit and enjoyed the time without a care in the world. The only place untouched by the holiday spirit was the Masisian home. Here everything went on as usual without the slightest change. Gayané and Hripsimé, dressed in their everyday clothes, went out for a walk in the garden after dinner.

Mrs. Masisian was in her room talking to a woman whose son Masisian had accused of reneging on a debt. The woman had come with tears in her eyes to plead her son's case, to beg Mrs. Masisian to use her influence with the agha to prevent her son from going to prison. "He's just a youngster without any experience in the world. He'll die of grief. His father left us with nothing but debt and we have nothing to live on. . ." she said. The poor woman kept on talking, pleading, crying. Mrs. Masisian was very upset there was nothing she could do to help, but said she couldn't possibly interfere in her husband's business. She told the woman that the best thing would be for her to go directly to Masisian and plead her case with him, but that he wasn't home at the moment.

Taking advantage of the holiday, Mikayel had gone for a walk with some acquaintances and returned to the house in quite good spirits. Seeing that the girls were in the garden, he went to join them at the edge of the pond where Gayané was tearing up pieces of bread to feed the fish. Hripsimé had rolled up her sleeves, revealing her lovely well-rounded arms, and was splashing the water around.

"Why didn't you go sing the *'Jan-Gyouloum'* with the neighbor's girls?" asked Mikayel as he walked up to them. "I swear, you really missed out. There were so many girls over there drawing lots in the Sarkhoshians' garden! Me and a few boys went over but they wouldn't let us in, the little devils. . ."

"Our father wouldn't let us go," answered Gayané sadly.

Seeing that Mikayel and her sister were so busily engaged in conversation and not paying her any attention, Hripsimé dipped a huge jug into the pond and filled it with water. She suddenly ran toward them and dumped the whole pitcher of water on Mikayel.

Mikayel was totally shocked, while Hripsimé stood back and laughed.

"Now you got a good bath! It had been too long." Meanwhile, Gayané was trying to comfort Mikayel and dry his clothes off with a cloth.

"Oh well, it's not so bad; after all, it's Vartavar and you can't get mad about a thing like that," said Gayané.

"No! It wasn't for Vartavar" said Hripsimé, still laughing heartily. "I got him wet so that he'd go and put on his new clothes. After all, it's a holiday. Doesn't he know any better?"

Mikayel suddenly felt ashamed for getting so upset with her prank.

"How did you know I had new clothes?" he asked.

"I know. . . And I know where you keep them. I'm going to go and get them right now," and so saying Hripsimé dashed off toward his little room which was close by. Mikayel ran after her to keep her from reaching his clothes and displaying them to everyone. Meanwhile Gayané, who couldn't catch up with them because of her lameness, kept calling to her sister to come back. But Hripsimé had already reached the 'junk closet' and was hastily rummaging around, looking for the clothes.

Mikayel grabbed hold of her hand and tried to restrain her, but she resisted. This turned into a protracted tugging match, and each time their hands touched or their heads brushed together a mysterious jolt ran through their tender nerves.

Mikayel finally gave in to Hripsimé's determination and let go of her.

"Why do you want me to get dressed up in my new clothes?" he asked.

"Because you'll look so good in them. . . so good," the young girl murmured almost inaudibly, her heartbeat pulsing in her voice.

"If that's why, then I'll put them on for you," said Mikayel with a smile.

"Well then. . . . Put them on. . . I'm leaving."

Hripsimé walked away from Mikayel's tiny room with flushed cheeks and eyes that glowed with an inexpressible joy.

As an older sister with a sense of responsibility, Gayané was offended by Hripsimé's brazen behavior with Mikayel and looked at her resentfully as she approached. But she trusted Mikayel because he had grown up in the home and could harbor only brotherly feelings towards Hripsimé. Yet she jealously noticed how Mikayel seemed happiest when talking to Hripsimé and how readily he had given in to her.

Gayané was as reserved and taciturn as Hripsimé was talkative and silly. Her handicap and the fact that she received little attention from the outside world may account for her more introspective nature. Girls in her position are generally morose and take a negative view of things, but Gayané was an exception; she was very kind-hearted. She displayed a special concern for Mikayel whose station in life was not so different from her own. Saying "this will be for Mikayel" she would always set aside a portion of her fruit dessert for him after dinner, occasioning an exchange of amused looks and laughter on the part of her mother, brother, and sisters. Her concern for this poor orphan had become a laughing matter. One evening at dinner time, when Gayané had thus set aside some dessert for Mikayel, the following typical exchange took place:

"She never forgets about her boy friend," commented Hripsimé.

"She's in love," said Stepan.

"I'm going to take her groom away from her," responded Hripsimé.

"Ah, how much fighting and hair pulling there will be between you two!" said Stepan.

Gayané usually took all of this in without uttering a word, but when they went too far tears welled up in her eyes. "I'm going to be an old maid. I don't need a groom. Let Hripsimé be happy. . ."

"Why should you be an old maid?" asked Stepan. "Wouldn't it be better to marry Mikayel and go settle with him in his village and tend the cows?"

"You're making fun of me again, Stepan," responded Gayané. "If that's the way you're going to be, then I'll never speak to Mikayel again," she said and started to leave with tears in her eyes.

Ms. Mariam listened in amazement to this squabble among her children. "Calm down, Gayané, there's nothing to get upset about. Mikayel's part of our family, not some outsider."

The fact that the two sisters were always confined to their home and never laid eyes on any young men outside its walls made it only natural for them to have feelings about Mikayel and discuss him. A few strains of these family disputes hadn't failed to reach Mikayel's ears and he thereafter kept his distance from the girls. Though these taunts had no really malicious intent but came from innocent and immature hearts, Mikayel nevertheless still retained his peasant boy's sense of shame.

Chapter 15

Special Marks

One day Masisian received a letter from one of his agents in Moscow. The man requested that Masisian send him an assistant because he wasn't feeling well and needed help managing the business. The letter caused quite a stir among Masisian's employees, since everyone wanted to be the man chosen for the job. But none of them met the qualifications specified in the letter. The letter made it clear that the assistant 'absolutely' had to know how to read, write, and speak Russian, in addition to Armenian. None of Masisian's store employees met these requirements, and he was quite worried about finding the right man.

One evening when Masisian returned home, instead of going inside as he usually did, he sat down on a bench in the shade of a walnut tree and asked Mikayel to bring him a glass of cold water to slake his thirst. Mikayel promptly brought the water, then stood by to respond to any further requests.

"Go tell Mrs. Masisian to come here," the agha commanded.

Within a few minutes Mrs. Masisian appeared and, like Mikayel, stood by waiting to comply with whatever her husband needed. The agha motioned her to sit down beside him, then told her about the letter. He asked her whom she thought he should send to Moscow. Mrs. Masisian was totally taken aback, this being the first time in their entire life together that he had asked her for advice. But she simply didn't have the experience to make such a judgement.

"That's for you to decide. Send whomever you think is best," she said.

Mikayel was nearby and had heard their discussion. He quickly decided on a proposal and stepped forward self-assuredly to present it:

"Send me, agha," he said.

Masisian frowned and was about to lose his temper, but then laughed despite himself.

"How would you know anything about a position like that, you little scamp?" said Masisian.

"I can read, write, and speak both Armenian and Russian," said Mikayel self-confidently.

"You? How could you have learned that?" asked the agha.

"Well, I did. . . And on my own. . ." he answered, prudently withholding the fact that Stepan had been his teacher.

Mr. and Mrs. Masisian just sat there stupefied, for they had no idea that he could read. And suddenly Mrs. Masisian was reminded of the problem that had worried her for such a long time, namely to get Mikayel out of the house before something developed between him and Hripsimé such as had developed with one of her other daughters who had fallen in love with a servant boy and run off to start a new life with him in his native village.

"Well, you don't have to look any further then," said Mrs. Masisian to her husband. "You won't find anyone better than Mikayel for the job. Let him go and become a man, this boy whom you've raised."

"Do you have a book in Russian?" asked the agha, turning to Mikayel.

"Yes."

"Then go and bring it here. I want to see you read from it."

So overjoyed at the opportunity, Mikayel rushed off to his room and bumped his head on the low door going in because he didn't bend down far enough. But he paid no attention to the pain and opened the box containing his sacred books, those given to him by Stepan. As he took one of them out he remembered what Stepan had said to him before his departure: "Read and read and never stop reading, Mikayel. It will help you someday," and now his words had come true. He wished with all his heart now to be off to Moscow to see his dear friend again.

Mikayel brought the book and stood before Masisian like a respectful pupil.

"Well then, read something and let's see," said Masisian.

Mikayel began the reading in a clear and confident voice. Masisian listened attentively though he couldn't understand a word.

"All right, now write something," said Masisian.

"What should I write?"

"Something like you'd write to my agent in Moscow: 'The last shipment of two hundred bales contains some of the purest American cotton plus a mix of the local type. The latter will be specially marked so that you can pass it off as the American.' Now – read it to me," Masisian commanded.

Mikayel did as he had been told.

"Did you put 'specially marked' in there?" asked the agha.

"Yes, 'The latter will be specially marked'" said Mikayel, reading again from what he had written. "But what if the buyer finds out what it really is?"

"Shut up, idiot! My man in Moscow is smarter than that, not like you. He knows how to handle things," said Masisian angrily. He then turned to his wife:

"You say I should send him, but how can I do such a thing when I know the little jackass will never turn into a real man."

But in reality no such cotton had been shipped, and this was all just a fantasy made up in Masisian's mind as a kind of joke to play on the market in Moscow.

Masisian insisted on blind acceptance of all his nefarious business practices, but now Mikayel had directly confronted him and provoked all his worst fears about him. Mikayel seriously regretted his brash comment and left even Ms. Mariam wondering about his judgement.

"It's all right. He's a bright boy – he'll go and see what needs to be done and learn," she said, in an attempt to save the situation.

"Goodness, learn what? If he hasn't learned after all these years, how's he going to start now?"

Mikayel just stood where he was and listened like a condemned man.

Just then a visitor appeared at the house, a man with a wide-brimmed hat and a stout homemade cane in his hand. He wore a dark threadbare coat with long full skirts and his soiled white stockings were exposed to view above his Persian slippers.

Mrs. Masisian and Mikayel were the first to notice him tapping his way toward them with his cane.

"Simon Hagorich is here!" they announced in unison.

Simon Hagorich was Masisian's attorney, an old police bureaucrat who had lost his job for drinking too much. He had come to see Masisian about the case of the young man whose mother had implored Mrs. Masisian to help keep her son out of debtors' prison.

"I was waiting for you. You arrived just in time," said Masisian.

"Of course, that woman is making such a fuss about her son," he said, settling down on the bench beside Masisian.

Simon Hagorich looked tired and unkempt. He took off his hat, wiped the sweat from his brow with his sleeve, then drew a large tin of snuff out of his pocket. After sucking a pinch of snuff up his gaping nostrils he brightened up a bit.

"I sued someone in court and won this from him just today. Try some, it's a blessing from heaven!" he offered.

"Just tell me how you handled that stupid woman," said Masisian, ignoring his offer.

"But please have some," the old attorney persisted. "I tell you, it's Stamboul's* finest. It took a lot of work to get it."

"Yes, I can see you're feeling really good now, Simon Hagorich. But tell me what you did about that conniving woman," Masisian insisted.

"Goodness, why get so upset?" said the attorney, taking a handkerchief to wipe some snuff particles from his tobacco stained moustache.

Masisian wagged his head. "Come on now and speak plainly: I said this, she said that. What came of it?"

"What do think? I cursed her out and put up whatever she had for sale."

Masisian's face lit up with delight at this news.

"And the money?" he asked.

"I have it here," said the attorney and with trembling fingers pulled a bundle of money wrapped in cloth out of his breast pocket and handed it to Masisian.

"Hey Mikayel, my boy, bring Simon Hagorich some *aragh*[*] in that big cup, you know the one I mean," Masisian said as he began to count the money.

"Well, it's about time! You know that Simon Hagorich can't do without that accursed potion," said the attorney, barely able to wait for the lifegiving beverage to arrive.

But Mikayel was fated to commit yet another of his serious blunders, just the sort that had aroused the agha's wrath so many times already: He failed to understand that when the agha told him to serve the aragh in the 'big' cup he really meant the small one. As a result, Simon Hagorich happily quaffed down the generous serving of pure, unmixed aragh.

"Ah-h-h, my heart is refreshed. Long life to you, young man!" said Simon Hagorich, gratefully handing the empty cup back to Mikayel. But Mikayel could see from the terrible scowl Masisian gave him that he had just made another of his big mistakes and suddenly despaired of ever being sent to Moscow.

In the mean time Mrs. Masisian was preoccupied with a very different train of thoughts, reflecting on the fact that all the 'conniving' widow's property had been taken away from her and sold and that her son had ended up in jail. Because of her husband's callousness an entire family would now be crushed and turned to dust in bitter poverty.

"Thank you, Simon Hagorich," said Masisian after he had finished counting the money, and he handed his attorney a ten rouble note. "This is your tip for helping me manage my money."

Simon Hagorich humbly accepted his 'tip' and came close to kissing Masisian's hand. Masisian was always quite liberal with his money in such situations, like a hunter who offers his dogs a tiny morsel of game to spur them on.

But Mikayel's dilemma still hadn't been resolved. Seeing what a good effect the money had on her husband's mood, Mrs. Masisian decided to take advantage of it to press Mikayel's case for going to Moscow.

"Please read this, and tell us if it's well written," she said as she handed Simon Hagorich the letter Mikayel had written down from dictation a few minutes earlier.

Simon Hagorich drew some large spectacles out of his breast pocket, put them on his massive nose and began reading the letter in a grave, oratorical manner: 'This time, a portion of the two hundred crates of cotton. . .' etc.

"Is 'special marks' written down there?" Masisian asked after Simon Hagorich had finished his reading.

"Of course it is: 'There are special marks on the latter crates . . .' and the words 'special marks' are underscored," replied the attorney.

"Is the writing good?" asked Masisian.

"Why, who wrote it?"

"Our young Mikayel here," said Masisian.

"I swear, his writing is better than mine, and I spent twenty-two years writing for the police and fifteen for the governor's office. But my writing still isn't worth a kopeck compared to his."

The generous serving of aragh had had its effect and this was his way of showing his appreciation to Mikayel. Nevertheless, this being an opinion offered by someone who knew what he was talking about, it went a long way to resolve the question in Mikayel's favor, and Masisian decided he would send Mikayel to Moscow after all.

Early in the morning three days later a carriage was waiting outside the Masisian house. Out came Mikayel dressed in his new suit and accompanied by Mr. and Mrs. Masisian. Mikayel went up to Mrs. Masisian to receive her maternal blessing, then kissed the agha's hand and received his final words of paternal counsel – which were points he had heard from him many times before. Mikayel mounted the carriage with an extremely bright and joyous look on his face, and the carriage pulled away from the house. As it was passing by the right wing of the house something fell into it from above, a bouquet of flowers. Mikayel looked up to see Gayané and Hripsimé standing on the roof nodding their heads to him. He was overjoyed, but one thing remained unclear: Which girl had thrown the flowers down? This question began to torment him.

END OF PART I

PART 2

Chapter 1

Moscow

Approximately one year had passed since Mikayel had set out for Moscow. It was Sunday, and in one of the older, run-down districts on the outskirts of Moscow, in a house that rented furnished rooms, a pale and sickly young man sat working at his writing table. Though it was well into the day, he hadn't washed up yet, and his thick, uncombed hair rested on his bare neck. Instead of a robe he wore an old overcoat, and instead of slippers he had on galoshes. The weather was grey and bitterly cold outside. The wind was driving clumps of snow against the frosted windows, making a mournful, dissonant sound. The room was unheated, but the young man didn't seem fazed by it. From time to time he would light his pipe as if to warm his frozen limbs.

Reminiscent of Dr. Faustus's[*] study, the large writing table was strewn with all sorts of things: papers, books, pamphlets; a pile of journals with a handful of pipe tobacco thrown on top; an assortment of beakers of various sizes that contained colorful powders and fluids; a number of implements related to chemistry and physics. There was also a human skull as well as some large chunks of coal which the young student evidently used in his experiments.

The room was quite bare – a few chairs, a bedstead, a lamp, a bookshelf, and that was it. This was home to a young man from the province of E and its most prosperous family, a poor student named Stepan Masisian.

There was a knock at the door and a maid entered.

"There's a gentleman here asking about you," she said.

"Let him come in," said Stepan casually without turning away from his work.

The visitor was a well dressed young man. Seeing before him a scholar sitting at his desk engrossed in his work, the young man paused awkwardly and stood where he was. Stepan looked up and was taken by surprise.

"Oh, Mikayel, is that really you? How you've changed! I barely recognized you," he said as he embraced his friend.

Mikayel couldn't manage a word.

"You in Moscow? What's going on? How did you get here?" Stepan asked, still holding Mikayel. "Come sit down and tell me your story."

The two of them sat down face to face and Mikayel explained the circumstances that had brought him to Moscow. He told Stepan that he had already been in Moscow for almost a year and had always hoped to see him but was prevented from doing so by Masisian's strict order to his Moscow agent that Mikayel was to be kept from having any contact with him lest Stepan 'ruin' him and cause him to 'take leave of his senses.' But the man he assisted had just died a few days earlier, and after taking care of his burial he had hurried to see Stepan.

"He was really a mean person. He'd keep an eye on my every move," added Mikayel.

"I didn't know him," said Stepan indifferently. "But what are you going to do now?"

Mikayel explained that he would be continuing the work the deceased man used to do. Because the air in Moscow was bad for his health, the man had requested some time off from his job so that he could go to his native town and recuperate, but Masisian had refused to give him the time. As a result, the man's health went into serious decline and soon thereafter he died.

"There's just one good side to all these changes. Now you'll stay here and I'll have the chance to continue teaching you. You haven't lost your love of reading have you, Mikayel," said Stepan.

"Oh, no!" said Mikayel with a pupil's humility. "I've never stopped reading all those books you gave me."

Mikayel was struck by the fact that Stepan hadn't mentioned a word about his family yet and asked him, "Have you received any letters from home?"

"No, and I don't want to," Stepan answered coolly. "What for? What could I expect to hear? Everything's the same as always, just the way I left it, isn't that true?"

"Yes, but don't you ever write to them?"

"No."

Mikayel was shocked by the poverty stricken state he found Stepan in. Still in the prime of youth, Stepan looked already exhausted and haggard, almost every ounce of his vitality having been drained away through constant, unbroken toil. There wasn't a bit of warmth in his room, a place that resembled the darkest of tombs, and his health was suffering for it.

A student is in a really terrible position, because he has to study and struggle against poverty at one and the same time. Instead of being able to focus completely on his field of study, he has to spend his most precious hours in the secondary pursuit of money in order to stave off starvation and survive. All of this was only too plain for Mikayel not to notice.

"What do you live on?" he asked.

"Oh, lots of things. I tutor children, I do translations, I work for a newspaper."

But by now Mikayel was experienced enough to know how Stepan's studying and health would surely suffer if he didn't take a rest from his secondary struggle for existence, at least for a couple of hours a day. He proposed to provide him with a modest sum every month to help out.

"Impossible!" replied Stepan.

"But why?"

"I don't need more money. Besides, you know very well that my father doesn't want me to get any of his money. You may try to keep it a secret, but it won't work, and when he finds out it could endanger your job."

"The money will come from my own pocket. I make more than I really need right now."

"You're going to need it later."

But Mikayel continued imploring Stepan to accept his proposal. He expressed his sense of obligation for all Stepan had done for him and said his refusal of the offer would make him very sad. And, he said, if he couldn't accept the money as a free gift, then he could pay it back in the future after he had finished his studies and had some money.

"It's hard, Mikayel, very hard," said Stepan.

"There's nothing hard about it at all. It's my own money, and I can do what I want with it."

"But that's not the problem. You have to understand that for my father nothing you have belongs to you. Even your own person is his property as long as you're under his control."

After their long talk together the two friends bid each other goodbye, the question of Mikayel's proposal remaining unresolved.

"You'll come see me again, won't you? I have some new books for you," said Stepan as he saw his friend off.

"Soon, very soon," said Mikayel.

Despite his best intentions and a heartfelt desire to help Stepan, Mikayel hadn't really come to terms with how difficult it would be to effect his plan, for in reality he didn't receive any pay. Masisian kept it in his own coffer to make it grow larger and larger.

Masisian had written to him: "Son, what are you going to do with the money if I give it to you? You'll just fritter it away and lose it all. This way it stays with me, and I take care of it so that it increases and finally amounts to a large fund that I can give you later." Mikayel didn't see how he could make an argument to receive a monthly salary, since all his basic needs – food, lodging, and clothing – were provided for him by the business.

Merchants in the East have always enjoyed an honorable status in the popular view. In Eastern tales and legends, 'khojas' have been as respected as caliphs for their purity and honesty. And Armenian merchants, being Asiatic businessmen, shouldn't have been devoid of the same honorable qualities as were found in the peoples with whom they had dealings, such as Persians, Assyrians, and especially Arabs.

And, in actuality, Armenian merchants still continue to practice many of those excellent customs, and they endure in their original and traditional forms among them. One of these customs is to adopt one's workers as apprentices. You'll see a boy – often from a poor, lower-class family, sometimes an orphan – taken on as a worker by a certain merchant. All it takes is for the merchant to recognize some special aptitude in the boy, whereupon he takes him under his special tutelage and guides him. The boy will be paid a wage, but instead of directly receiving it his employer saves it for him and sees to it that it grows until such time as the boy is sufficiently advanced in the trade to be set up in his own business. The merchant for whom he has worked will then give him the total of the wages he has earned over the years of his apprenticeship, plus a free sum on top of it. With this additional money the young man will have the capital to make a go of his new business. Furthermore, he receives a line of credit from his former employer which then goes to helping him expand his business. Employees of this sort are called 'the agha's adoptees'. The agha thus receives honor and respect from society for helping to make 'a man' out of a former employee, and such a man is known as the 'light' of the agha, that is, the light of hope that the agha has kindled in the heart of some impoverished family on hiring their son, and the more such 'lights' the agha has lit in his community, the greater his esteem.

But Masisian took a more utilitarian view of this tradition. In his case he used it to bind the employee to himself and keep him under his complete control. Keeping the employee's salary in his own hands, he used it to ensure his complete subservience; for with the slightest sign of disobedience he could dismiss him and keep the whole sum for himself as a penalty. He would even accuse a totally innocent man of insubordination and cut off his pay. This was why there was such a high turnover in the people who worked for him.

On returning home after his visit with Stepan, Mikayel sat down and wrote a letter to Masisian asking to receive his pay on a monthly basis so that he could try his luck buying lottery tickets. Masisian refused and said this would be a very foolish thing for him to do; that he himself was Mikayel's good fortune; that he was all the help

Mikayel needed, and that he should follow his advice so that he could become a respectable 'man'. Mikayel was very angry at this response and was all prepared to write back and tell him that if he didn't agree with his wishes he would quit his job. But he didn't write any such letter. Despite the fact that he was completely familiar with Masisian's personality and had no faith at all in any of his promises, he couldn't quit his job; not because of the money he would forfeit, no. There was something else that bound him as closely to Masisian's family as he was to the business, something very special, for he hadn't forgotten the bouquet of flowers that had been dropped into his carriage on leaving the Masisian home years before . . .

Chapter 2

A Helping Hand

Mikayel's room wasn't far from the Moscow bourse,[*] in the home of a poor German family who provided services for him. The clean and orderly furnishings of his little room were a complete reflection of Mikayel's moderate personality, and he felt entirely at ease there. He would sometimes sit at his window looking out on the multifarious crowds of people flowing through the streets and the rows of great houses, imagining himself to be in a new, enchanted world. It was in moments like these that his thoughts often turned to his homeland, wandering far, far away to the banks of the Arax, picturing himself there with his shepherd's staff in hand, sandals on his feet, a large hide cap on his head and driving his sheep to lush green pastures. What a great gulf separated that past and his present, what a difference between Kalo the shepherd boy and Mikayel the hero of the Moscow bourse!

Stepan appeared at his door one evening with a large batch of books. He set them down on the table and sank into the armchair. Though he seemed extremely tired, his face was beaming with joy. Mikayel told him how Masisian had responded to his proposal for receiving his pay.

"What did you expect? I could have told you that," said Stepan contemptuously. "But never mind, come here, I want to show you the books I brought."

Mikayel went to the table and started looking over the books with a student's curiosity.

"From this one you'll learn something about finance and banking," said Stepan as he flipped through its pages. "From this other one you'll find out about the main commodities produced in different countries. The third book will introduce you to factories and manufacturing. But this fourth one is an outstanding novel. When you start to get bored with the other books, this is the one to read. It'll cultivate your mind and develop your taste."

The books were so new their pages hadn't been cut yet. Mikayel took them in his hands, looked at them, then set them back down on the table.

"I forgot to mention that I received permission for you to attend the business school twice a week," said Stepan. "Will you have the time?"

"Twice a week?" said Mikayel thinking it over. "Why not? Sure I can."

"Very good, then I'll be here early tomorrow morning to take you and introduce you to the administrator," said Stepan as he prepared to leave. "So, until then. I'll be here at eight o'clock."

"But what's your hurry?" said Mikayel. "Stay awhile. I was just going to make tea."

"I can't, I have several places to go," said Stepan, and he left.

"How good he is," thought Mikayel after his friend had left. "But he's as proud as he is good. I won't accept his help for free. Our situations are very similar: he's poor in money and I'm poor in education. We need to complement each other. If he doesn't let me help him at all, I'll be very hurt and won't accept his concern for me, either. But how can I help him . . . ?

This latter question threw Mikayel into torment. He wanted to do the right thing by Stepan and could easily provide him with four or five thousand roubles out of the business budget without his father ever finding out. On the other hand he wanted the money to come out of his own pocket, but because Masisian insisted on keeping both him and his money tightly in his own hands, he didn't have it.

"I'll have to show that old fool that I don't need his money and that I can earn my money elsewhere," he thought as he went to his table and sat down to write a letter.

By this time Mikayel had earned such a name for himself in the bourse for his competence and he enjoyed such prestige among his fellow merchants that many of them who didn't have assistants offered him work to do for them on commission. He calculated that he could thus earn a good sum and wrote his letter in a way that made that fact perfectly clear to Masisian. The style and content of this letter reflected none of the timorousness of a mere worker, but the thoughts of a free and independent man. He made it clear that he was receiving proposals from left and right asking him to take work on commission. He said that he was perfectly capable of accepting all that work without in the least compromising the interests of Masisian's business. He stated that he would take a certain percentage for himself and render the rest to Masisian for his own needs. He concluded his letter by saying that in case Masisian refused his offer, he would be forced to quit his position and become a free agent.

Masisian was initially upset with this letter, this being the first time any of his workers had dared to be so frank with him, but what could he do?

His business was at a critical juncture. "I knew that damned son of mine would corrupt him," he muttered, sure that Stepan would have established contact with Mikayel to get money from him after his Moscow agent had died.

But when he had reflected further on Mikayel's proposal, his sense of irritation subsided, for he was the sort of man for whom the profit motive outweighed every other consideration. Therefore, why should he lose out on this opportunity? On the other hand, he didn't like the idea of Mikayel becoming his own man, for he wanted to keep his workers poor in order to ensure their obedience to him. How could he reconcile this contradiction? That was the question. He concluded that he simply couldn't sacrifice his interests and be left high and dry. That would be impossible. Mikayel had made it quite clear that if his proposal was denied he would quit his position and go into business for himself. Losing an employee of Mikayel's caliber would be a serious hardship, for who could take his place? There wasn't anyone. So reluctantly Masisian agreed to Mikayel's proposal, leaving the matter of punishing him for another day . . .

The agha's letter to Mikayel was as moderate as Mikayel's had been firm, expressing his paternal happiness that he had developed so much and wishing him more success to come. He said that he took pride in the fact the boy he had shaped had finally become a 'man', and finished by advising Mikayel to invest his earnings in the business rather than keeping them for himself. That way, the agha would add his money to his already saved salary and it would thus collect considerable interest.

On reading these final lines, Mikayel smiled and said, "You won't be tricking me any more. I know you too well."

Chapter 3

The Devil's Workshop

Mikayel's workload now became heavier. He was taking on many jobs from other merchants, attending classes at the business school twice a week, visiting various businesses to see how they operated, and spending all his time at home studying. He thus had little time to relax. His lifestyle was so alien to the other Armenian merchants that he became the object of general gossip and jealous slander among them. Several of them took it upon themselves to write to Masisian and inform him of the 'delinquency' his employee had fallen into; but since at the beginning of the new year Mikayel had turned over five thousand roubles to Masisian, after taking his commission, Masisian paid no attention to these treacherous reports. Mikayel only received a thousand roubles for his salary, while he had made five thousand, so how could Masisian fail to be pleased? And even if he wanted to, he had no way of putting any pressure on Mikayel, since he had now established an independent position for himself.

There were all sorts of Armenian merchants in Moscow: from Ashdarak,* Nor Nakhichevan, Tiflis, Gharabagh,* Yerevan, Agoulis, even Tabriz.

You would find them at any hour of the night or day in front of the bourse, even if it was closed and there wasn't any business going on. Like a wandering brahmin, the Armenian merchant never parts from that temple of commerce and derives particular pleasure from gazing at its sealed doors. But Mikayel was never there after midday and the close of business, something that the other merchants seriously resented and attributed to arrogance on his part. Nevertheless,

Mikayel naturally eschewed this chattering, idle crowd, these men who had nothing else to do, who never left their narrow Armenian circle, who passed all their time with crass joking and tawdry gossip. The Armenian merchant has no idea how to structure his time so that when it's time to work he works, then in his leisure hours he devotes himself to learning something new. He has no interest in any group outside his narrow Armenian world. That's why he always remains one-sided, coarse, uncultivated, and when he returns home, no matter where he's been, he brings back with him the same mentality, the same feelings, the same character as he had before he left.

In Moscow, as everywhere, Armenians from certain places harbored strong animosities toward Armenians from other places, for instance, Gharabaghtsis toward Zoks,[*] Zoks toward Tiflistsis, and so on. Even Armenians from the same town were hostile to their fellow citizens, for instance the Ashdaraktsis. All of them were prepared to do the others in, even if they lost money doing it. There was no sincerity in their words, and though they put on a big show of friendship they all tried to trick each other every chance they got. An empty and idle life had turned all of them into parasites who fed off each other.

You'll see a throng of Armenian merchants gathered in front of the bourse dressed in every kind of Asiatic or European clothing, talking away loudly, laughing and guffawing, telling each other little anecdotes that stereotype people from certain towns or provinces, all the while totally oblivious of the unbecoming image they project in public. And thus, a Zok with a wily face and shifty eyes was once heard telling the following story to his fellow Armenian merchants in front of the Moscow bourse:

"Listen to this, it was Palm Sunday and we had gone to church. When the liturgy was over we went out into the churchyard and were standing around listening to a conversation some ladies were having. Before we knew it, there came a bunch of Zoks over to greet Mr. N., a Gharabaghtsi. They took hold of his hand and started shaking it, congratulating him the whole time, saying 'Happy name day! Happy name day!' over and over again. 'What are you talking about? This isn't my name day,' the Gharabaghtsi said, totally taken aback. 'But of course it is! Don't you know that this is the day Jesus Christ rode the donkey into Jerusalem?' said one of the Zoks."

The crowd of merchants broke out into hearty laughter at this sorry attempt at wit and equating Gharabaghtsis with donkeys, but there was a Gharabaghtsi among them and he took offense:

"You're mistaken. You have no reason to slur us Gharabaghtsis like that," said he. "We Gharabaghtsis are the most intelligent Armenians of all, even if we're not as devilish as the Zoks. But the devil himself can fall feet first into a trap, you know. Let me tell you a little story about a Zok that took place right here one time."

"Let's hear it! Let's hear it!" everyone shouted.

"This Zok was about to sell a hundred bales of cotton to a Russian buyer one day," the Gharabaghtsi began. "To prove the quality of his merchandise, he opened up a few bales of his finest and showed it to the Russian, but a fellow Zok – in true Zok fashion – betrayed him to the Russian and tipped him off that the entire load wasn't necessarily as fine as what he had seen. So the Russian insisted on taking a closer look at several of the other bales and, O my God, what a frightful mess he found! Inside them were broken brooms, fragments of wooden spoons, worn-out shoes, odds and ends of rugs, and – lo and behold – from one of them came spilling out an enormous donkey blanket. This was a bit much for the Russian. 'I assume that used to be your father's overcoat,' he said to the Zok, pointing at the donkey blanket. Without so much as blushing the Zok replied, 'I'll have you know, my father came from a very wealthy family. How else do you think I got all this merchandise?'"

The Zoks found themselves quite disconcerted by the Gharabaghtsi's story, yet persisted in trying to justify their countryman's behavior, pressing their case that if his ruse had succeeded – worthless donkey blanket and all – he would have made off with a huge killing. They then launched into a whole string of further tales to prove their point about the simplicity of the Gharabaghtsis.

"There was once a big hail storm," one of them began. "Some Gharabaghtsi peasants got together to decide what they should do. They agreed, 'Whatever becomes of our crops, so be it. Let's at least go and save the landlord's crop.' So they all went to their houses and grabbed blankets, rugs, cloaks, and whatever else they could find and ran off to the landlord's estate to shield his crop, but as they were doing so they trampled it all to the ground. Now, if that's not truly asinine I don't know what is!"

And so it went. . . . This was the kind of rubbish our merchants indulged in every day, whiling away their afternoon hours in front of the Moscow bourse. But Mikayel was never found among them.

Chapter 4

Secret Agenda

The Armenian merchants in Moscow generally kept their distance from the numerous Armenian students there, even if they were friends or close relatives. The students often took their money without ever thinking of paying it back, and the merchants hated them for their gay and idle lifestyle. The only merchant who had anything to do with them was Mikayel, and he had become acquainted with many of them through Stepan. Like his uncle Aved, called 'Brother' by his respectful peasant neighbors, Mikayel enjoyed a similar respect among the students. If it were a matter of a charitable function or helping out a poor or sick student, the students would say, 'Let's ask Brother Mikayel for help. He'll get the merchants to donate something.' One night Mikayel's room was unusually animated with a gathering of young merchants who were there smoking and talking. The weak light of a lamp barely lit up the gloomy interior, a gloom made thicker by the tobacco smoke and steam from the samovar. Mikayel was serving tea to his guests.

"Say what you will, it's always dreary in your place," said one of his guests.

"What makes you say that?" asked Mikayel with a smile.

"Because, there's never any card games or backgammon."

"Go ahead and play; no one's preventing you."

"How can we play if you don't?"

"Then I'll play."

"But it's going to be for money."

"And for big money, too," chimed in another of the guests.

"Why does it have to be for money when the point is just to have a good time?" said Mikayel.

"Who has time just to play around. We play for thousands every night."

The door opened and the conversation came to a halt. A young man standing in the door said to his friends, "Let's go in. We found them at last and there's a lot of them."

Three students entered the room. One of them placed a sheet of paper on the table. Turning to Mikayel's guests he addressed them in a formal manner:

"Gentlemen, this fundraising appeal is for a very noble purpose, and any Armenian who still has a bit of feeling in his heart for our brothers in Turkish Armenia and all the exploitation and suffering they've been forced to endure won't fail to help. This is why I ask each of you to sign this document and contribute as much as you can."

You would think that someone had poured cold water over the gentlemen's heads.

"Eh! They're getting very tedious with their list of signatures," said one man, turning his head away.

"We are here, the Turkish Armenians are there. We can't even take care of our own kids properly," said another.

Another gentleman asked suspiciously, "What did you say the signatures are for?"

The students were stymied for a moment, then one of them spoke up:

"It's clear you don't care about it, and since you've given our appeal such a cold reception, I don't think you need any more details," he said in a very offended tone.

Mikayel said nothing. The indifference of his guests was only too obvious.

The students prepared to leave and Mikayel saw them to the door.

"There you have it; so much for our capitalists, our material strength. How can we expect anything from these heartless corpses?" remarked one of the students.

"Oh go to hell!" said one of the guests.

On reaching the top of the stairs which led down to the entrance, Mikayel asked, "What are the signatures for?"

The students became absorbed in thought for several moments, after which one of them answered:

"It's a secret . . . But we don't need to keep it from you . . . You're one of our own . . . You're aware that one of the emissaries[*] for the Patriarch of Constantinople is already in St. Petersburg and the other one is in London. The position of the Armenians in Turkey is suspended by the thinnest thread, and it's time to get to work. We're getting ready to send a young man abroad to be a propagandist in the European press."

Mikayel beamed with happiness at this.

"That's a really great idea. Who is it going to be?"

"Your friend, Mr. Masisian."

"Strange he never mentioned it to me."

"He's very closemouthed. He didn't want you to find out until he'd left."

"That's fine. But just tell him to come by and see me before he leaves and I can give him whatever he still needs for his trip."

The students shook hands with Mikayel and left. Returning to his guests Mikayel found them still vociferously condemning and heaping ridicule on the students.

"They must have blown all their pocket change," said one of the guests.

"Yes, here they are starving, but they're all worried about folks in Turkey," said another.

"They're pestering us all the time, these beggars," said another guest. "They never know when to call it quits, for heaven's sake! The other day they came up and asked me to contribute for the Alashgertsi refugees.[*] Boy, did I blow up when I heard that – I really gave them a piece of my mind. I told them, 'Get out of here – you and your poor Alashgertsis!'"

At this point Mikayel couldn't take any more:

"It's impossible to be so cold-blooded about the national agenda! Every Armenian has to do his part. We have money – that's what we can give. The students are educated and they know how to use words

– that's their contribution. Other people are brave and strong – they can lend their muscle. No Armenian should hold back anything he has! If everyone does his part, only then will the Turkish Armenians at last be able to breathe freely again."

"Great, great," said one of his guests, interrupting him. "Enough of these national concerns, let's think about ourselves. Bring the cards so we can play."

"To tell you the truth, I don't feel at all like playing right now," said Mikayel.

"Which is to say, 'Get up and leave.' Well, we didn't come here to listen to sermons," said one of Mikayel's guests as he stood up.

"If my place has been so boring to you, please go ahead and leave. No one's forcing you to stay."

Most of his guests left resentfully, only two of them staying behind.

These were two young merchants who were the type of men who, though they have a modicum of intelligence, pull their punches and keep their mouths shut when around men of a higher class because of their inherited deference to authority; this even when the latter advanced ideas that were erroneous and harmful. But now finding themselves alone with Mikayel, their tongues loosened up.

"Oh, what deadened and unfeeling hearts those men have!" said one of them. "Nothing concerns them, nothing interests them if it's outside the realm of their profits or their work. The idea of a nation, of a compatriot, of all humankind means nothing to them as long as they can't gain some advantage from it, and they look at everything from a commercial point of view."

Mikayel was quite excited by now and stood up from his place on the divan to say something:

"If only they had an idea what it takes to be normal businessmen, but I assure you they don't. No, the old generation did better in the way they handled their business. The only distinction the new merchants have is wearing western clothes instead of Asiatic robes like their grandfathers, but the Europeans are smarter. The old merchants were uneducated and their business skills were limited, but at least they had the sense not to try and do business with people who were better at it than they were. They preferred trading with less developed people so they could cheat them. But the new generation doesn't understand how cunning the Europeans are. They go right out and do business with them and they lose out every time."

Mikayel's opinions were a bit much for one of his young guests: "Nevertheless, there are exceptions," he said.

"The exceptions are trivial," answered Mikayel. "If they still have any wealth left, that came from their fathers and grandfathers, but they don't know how to keep it. I could mention any number of trading houses that have gone bankrupt in just the last few years, especially when their sons took up trade with more developed countries. For instance, almost all of them who started trading with Marseille and Manchester got wiped out, but in Russia they were able to sustain themselves and even do well. That's only because Russian merchants are no further advanced than the Armenians and in some cases they're not as skillful."

This was the first time that Mikayel's guests had heard such ideas, and they fell into reflection.

"There's a general lack of what's called commercial science among us," continued Mikayel. "Our merchants enter into the market almost half consciously, without thought or preparation. Everyone just follows the other's example. One man starts buying cotton, and right away the others start buying it without any direct knowledge of their own. One man starts buying silk, and right away a whole group follows in his steps. If you ask those gentlemen why they're buying it or where they plan to sell it they'll tell you, Giragos and Mardiros buy it, so why shouldn't we? We're just as good as they are."

"That's really true," observed one of the guests and Mikayel continued:

"The one legacy of their forefathers the new generation have fully preserved is cheating in all its forms. The practice of business quickly degenerates when it's based solely on deception. Right now, Europeans and Russians have a very low view of Armenian goods like cotton, wool, or even silk, because they see that they so often come mixed up with all kinds of stuff. Nobody trusts us. They won't buy anything from us before they've opened it up and taken a good look;

whereas Europeans, for example, will sell hundreds of sealed bales to each other, and they're all of the same high quality."

Mikayel went on at great length about various mercantile shenanigans and the corrupt practices in which Armenian merchants were mired. He made the point that their corruptness has a negative effect on all Armenians, because other people form their opinions of Armenians from our merchants who travel to every corner of the globe. Only because of this handful of unsavory characters, the rest of the world is left with a negative image of Armenians, whereas in reality the great majority of Armenians, made up mostly of artisans and agriculturists, are decidedly decent and moral people.

"So consider – What good can come of these unscrupulous, immoral men to whom nothing is sacred? And yet we're shocked and angry to see how callous they are toward their brothers suffering beneath the yoke of Islam," said Mikayel in conclusion.

It was by now already past midnight. Mikayel's last two guests had finally gone and he was left alone. He was very perturbed and, try as he might, couldn't get to sleep. He paced back and forth silently in his room, totally absorbed in thinking about Stepan. That inspired yet reticent young man had now accepted a role in the most relevant and crucial undertaking possible, one that Mikayel fully supported. But why had he kept it from him? Mikayel wondered. Wasn't he trustworthy or reliable enough? Didn't he deserve to know? 'No', he thought at last, 'It was out of pride he kept it from me, that impossible pride of his. He recoils from a helping hand as from a snake about to strike. But to act that way with me?. . . . . That really hurts!'

Chapter 5

The Telegram

Mikayel lived as a lodger in an apartment belonging to a poverty-stricken German widow. The apartment consisted of two rooms and a kitchen. The widow and her family lived in one room, and Mikayel lived in the other. There weren't any men left in the widow's family and the entire economic burden of the household had fallen on her shoulders. Her daughter Ida, who had two little children to feed, did everything she could to help. The widow's husband had been a tailor and after his death his entire business had been sold off to pay his debts. Now Ida was forced to take in sewing from French clothing shops to make ends meet, and her mother helped her with the work. The rent they received from Mikayel therefore went a long way to relieving their straitened circumstances. In exchange they provided him with a furnished room, did his cooking and cleaning, and generally looked after his daily needs.

One morning Mikayel was sitting at his writing table hurriedly writing letters which he needed to mail soon. Ida brought some coffee for him and set it down on the small round table.

"Will you be going out soon?" she asked.

"Why do you ask?"

"Because I wanted to put your room in order, and I won't have time later on."

"I still have five or six letters to write, but you can do whatever you were going to do."

"But I might disturb you."

"Not at all . . . Quite the contrary," said Mikayel.

Ida was a tall, elegant young lady, with luxuriant red hair and a bright, pleasant face. Her lovely blue eyes had all the light and beauty of the azure sky. She seemed happier than usual this morning, and though Mikayel was occupied, she frequently interrupted him with various questions.

"Ah, how sloppy you are! Nothing's in order here and the floor is covered with things," the young lady said as she went about the room straightening things up.

"I'll try to be neater for you from now on," said Mikayel with a smile.

"It's not such a problem. It's just that I like to see your room in decent order," the young lady said, blushing a little.

"You're very nice, Ida."

The young lady had finished her job and going up behind Mikayel placed her hand on his shoulder. She bent over to look at his writing and saw how swiftly his pen was flying over the white stationery.

"What topsy-turvy writing that is!" she said as she shifted her position and looked at a finished letter lying on the table. "How many of them do you write a day?"

"Ten or more."

"So that's why you stay up all night."

"How do you know?"

"I do . . . Lots of times I notice that the light doesn't go out in your room until dawn, and I hear you pacing around. I don't get much sleep either. . ."

Mikayel didn't respond. The young lady seemed embarrassed by her candid remarks and picked up one of the letters to look at it.

"I can't make this writing out at all; it's not like any language I've ever seen before, but it's very beautiful. I wouldn't at all mind learning the script and language that you write in."

"What would you do with it?" asked Mikayel.

"It might be useful some day . . ." the young lady replied with a bright smile, then suddenly rushed out of the room without looking back as if ashamed of what she had said.

Mikayel felt disturbed and stopped writing for several moments. The poor girl, he thought with considerable discomfort, how would

I be able to help her with what her heart needs? Mikayel had long ago noticed how interested Ida was in him and how many nights, when he was occupied with his work, she approached his window to see if the lodger was awake or not. Mikayel had attributed this behaviour to a young girl's burning curiosity about every little thing, as she might be curious about what her mother kept locked up in a special place. But today she had clearly given her feelings away in a way that Mikayel couldn't have expected. She had expressed a desire to learn the language and script that belonged to Mikayel's nationality, with the thought that 'it might be useful some day'. . . Ida wasn't joking, for she was a quite serious young lady. Her wish to learn the Armenian language and writing was so that she could love an Armenian. And who would that Armenian be? It was Mikayel that she loved, but how could he respond to her love? That was the thought that now tormented him.

Mikayel had no corresponding feeling in his heart toward the beautiful young lady's love. He only honored her as a dutiful young woman, a hard working girl who had taken on so much responsibility for the survival of her unfortunate family. Mikayel could like her. But love her? Hardly.

He wasn't even sure if he had properly finished his letters but quickly put them in envelopes, sealed them with wax and was about to take them out when, all of a sudden, Stepan showed up. He extended his hand to Mikayel in the same calm, cool manner as always, then settled into the armchair he always used when visiting him.

"I came to see you about something very serious," he said flatly.

"I know," said Mikayel. "I've already heard about what you're going to do, and you can count on my support for whatever you need for your trip abroad."

"That's not it, read this telegram" said Stepan calmly.

Mikayel began reading the long message that ran for over twenty lines and immediately went pale. It was addressed to Stepan and contained the following lines: "Your father met his end due to a sudden stroke. Hurry and don't lose a moment in getting here. His business is in a total mess. We'll soon lose everything we have if something isn't done about it. Get hold of all the business records that Mikayel has and close the Moscow business,' etc.

Signed, 'Mariam'."

Mikayel sat frozen in place. To him it was even clearer than it could have been to Stepan what the frightful consequences might be.

"I'm prepared to immediately turn all the business records over to you. Just hurry and get back," Mikayel said, taking several large record books out of a cabinet.

"But I'm getting ready to go abroad," said Stepan with his usual coolness. "I'm being called abroad by a higher duty than my father's business."

"I agree," said Mikayel, "But you have to consider that your whole family's future is at stake here. Think of your mother and your sisters – and yourself as well. The message is quite clear: your whole inheritance is in jeopardy. I know how your father handled his business – he kept all his accounts in his own head. Now that he's gone, that's all gone with him, and his crooked assistants have everything in their clutches. It's clear how things will turn out . . ."

"As the saying goes, what comes with the flood is carried off by the flood," said Stepan philosophically. "How could it be otherwise ? My father's the one who trained them, after all . . ."

Clearly aware of the disaster that Stepan's obstinacy might very well lead to, Mikayel forcefully tried again to persuade his friend to respond to his mother's urgent and heartfelt plea.

"Wouldn't it be better for you to postpone your trip until this business is taken care of?" he asked.

"That's impossible."

"Then what are we going to do?"

"That's what brought me here, Mikayel. Listen, my mother's plea means little to me compared with the appeal of thousands of mothers in Turkey who are calling out for help. I'm going, and I'll travel all over Europe to do what I can. As for my father's business, in a critical moment like this I have just one friend to depend on and that's you. I'm placing all my hope on you; in any case, you're better qualified to take care of those affairs than I am. You'll have an authorization letter from me and soon be on your way. Agreed?"

Seeing that there was no alternative and that his friend's entire inheritance was in danger of being lost to dishonest players, Mikayel agreed to the arrangement.

"Then there's not a moment to lose," said Stepan happily. "Let's go to a notary right away so that you'll have the papers you need."

That night Mikayel began gathering up his belongings and packing his suitcase, all the while preoccupied with what he would tell Ida and how to approach it. He knew that the poor girl would be very sad when she learned he was leaving. But it was no less difficult for him to leave that good and peaceful home that he had grown so used to, where he had spent so many enjoyable hours and found such tender solicitousness. But where was Ida? Usually by this hour she would have come in to serve tea.

Ida's mother entered Mikayel's room.

"Where have you been, sir?" she asked, casting an inquisitive eye at his open suitcase. "You've been keeping us waiting for quite a while at the table."

"I was busy," said Mikayel. "But where's Ida? I haven't seen her today."

"She's not feeling her best today," said the old woman anxiously. "First thing this morning she complained of a headache. She hasn't had anything to eat or drink all day, and now she's sleeping. Lord, how will we get along if she gets sick?" she said pitifully as tears welled in her eyes framed by the deep wrinkles of her face. Mikayel was deeply affected by her words and decided to summon a doctor immediately.

"It seems you're getting ready to go somewhere, sir," she observed after feeling a bit better.

"Yes, mama, I'm getting ready to go back to my homeland."

"When?"

"Right away, tomorrow morning."

The poor old woman was overwhelmed.

"That'll be hard for us, very hard," she said in a trembling voice. "It won't be easy for us to see you go. We've all got so used to each other. We love you like a son, and now you're going to leave."

"Who knows, I may be back quite soon," said Mikayel to comfort her.

"Godspeed to you, son. Go and bring joy to your parents."

The old lady didn't know that Mikayel didn't have any parents and had been an orphan since childhood.

"But what can we do for Ida?" asked Mikayel. "She seems very sick and she needs a doctor."

"Only God knows, son. She doesn't say anything, that's the way she is. I can see that she's as pale as an autumn leaf, but she won't tell me where she hurts and she just puts up with her sickness. She stays on her feet all the time, and she won't stop working."

"Can I go in and see her?"

"Why not? Let's go."

The old woman led Mikayel into the adjoining room. The girl's bed was curtained off, and she had lain down without even getting out of her clothes. Her mother pulled the curtain aside, and the lamp light fell on her feverish face which was glowing with an inexplicable fire.

Mikayel felt a shudder go through him, and he asked, "What's happened to you, Ida?"

"Oh, nothing," she answered in a feeble voice. "I just have a little temperature. I have a headache, but it'll go away. It's happened many times before."

She laid her head back down on the pillow as if to convey that she simply wanted to rest. Her mother released the curtain, and the girl was hidden once more behind the ominous partition.

"She's seriously ill. I'm going to send for a doctor immediately," said Mikayel to Ida's forlorn mother. "But make sure you don't let her know that I'm leaving in the morning," he added.

"I know . . . I know all about it . . ." came Ida's feeble voice from behind the curtain, followed by heartrending sobs.

Mikayel didn't pay any attention and left quickly, while Ida's mother went back to comfort her.

The doctor arrived a half hour later and said that Ida's illness wasn't grave. He said it was just a slight fever that would pass with proper care, but that she shouldn't be left alone, otherwise it could get worse. He left after issuing instructions and writing some prescriptions.

Now it was up to Mikayel to hurry off to the pharmacy for medicine, for there was no one else in the house to do it.

Ida passed the night in delirium, with her mother and Mikayel at her side the entire time. When morning came she finally felt better and fell asleep.

"You can go now, sir. She's fallen asleep," said Ida's mother in a barely audible voice. "I'm grateful for your generosity, but now it's time for you to go and get ready for your trip.

On returning to his room, Mikayel began restlessly pacing back and forth. Never in his life had he been in such a helpless and impossible position as this. Two emotions battled within him: On one side was the heavy responsibility his dear friend Stepan had placed on him. The fate of the Masisian family now depended on him alone, and the slightest carelessness could result in their being deprived of their daily bread. On the other side, Ida was lying sick in bed, and leaving her in that desperate state was a very difficult thing to do.

How could he resolve this dilemma, this choice between his love for a friend and love for a woman? Which was more important? And did he really love her? He had lived here for all of five years, and never once had he been troubled by such a feeling, and never once had Ida given him the slightest impression that she loved him. But from the night he found out that she was sick and heard her crying from behind the bed curtain because he was leaving, when a certain unexplainable feeling began to stir in his heart. What was it – love, deceitful passion, or the compassion he always felt toward sufferers who held out their hands for help? Mikayel couldn't say, for he hadn't had enough experience yet to make sense of such dark, inscrutable matters of the soul.

Many hours passed as sleeplessly he paced about his little room preoccupied with grave, disquieting reflections, until at last he heard the morning bells ringing from the churches. The night had slipped by unnoticed.

Suddenly his eyes fell on his suitcase which was fully packed and ready to go. It seemed that this mute, inanimate object began to speak to him, began to affect him, began to communicate to him an absolute obligation which he couldn't evade. This was the same suitcase that he had loaded into the carriage on leaving the Masisians' house, and now it reminded him of that bouquet of flowers that the two sisters had dropped down from the roof as he was pulling away . . . And all of a sudden, before his mind's eye he saw the image of Gayané's and Hripsimé's delicate faces.

Just at that moment there was a clamor of carriage wheels in the street, and within a few minutes the driver was at the door.

"Sir, you asked for me to come early in the morning, so I apologize for being a bit late," he said with a bow of his head.

"That's fine, just take that suitcase out, then wait for me a bit. I won't be long," said Mikayel after a moment's reflection.

The carriage driver was the same man that Mikayel had hired on the night he went out to get a doctor for Ida, and he had told him to come early the following morning to take him to the train station.

The moment of truth had arrived. After a few moments of hesitation, Mikayel went to the table, took a sheet of paper, and wrote the following lines:

"Farewell to you, Ida. Please accept this small gift as a token of brotherly love. It will help you through in your time of need, when you're ready to set your own future in order. . ."

He signed it, placed a thick stack of money with it, then sealed it with wax and left the room. Going into the other room, he found Ida's mother still sitting near her daughter's bed.

"I've come to say goodbye, madam," he said to Ida's mother.

"So you're going already!" said the old woman, quite flustered. "Shall I wake Ida up?"

"Don't disturb her, it might not be good for her."

"Akh, how sad she'll be when she wakes up and finds you gone!"

"Ida's very good, and she'll forgive me for the discourtesy," said Mikayel, as he reached into his breast pocket and pulled out the thick letter he had prepared. "Please give this letter to her."

Mikayel went to see Ida one last time. He found her lying in bed with her luxuriant hair falling across her face, her lips parted as if talking sweetly to someone and one hand hanging down from the covers as if offered in a pledge of eternal friendship. He tenderly took her hand, pressed it to his lips, and taking one last look at the beautiful young woman left the room.

Ida's mother accompanied him to the door, gave him her blessing and saw him off.

That same morning a group of students in another part of the city gathered to say farewell to another young who was embarking on a journey to England. They kissed him goodbye and as he was boarding the train they said, "Go, child of the fatherland, and may the spirit of Vartan* and Nerses* be with you . . ."

Chapter 6

One Golden Feather

Bedros Masisian's sudden death was a terrible blow to his unfortunate family. Mrs. Masisian, forlorn and beside herself, had no idea what to do. The family didn't have one good friend. Masisian's alienating, negative, and self-centered nature had so isolated him that there was no one left to give his inexperienced family some friendly advice on how to deal with the property he had left behind. As for Mrs. Masisian, she was intelligent enough and understood things, but she had been placed in such a positon over the years by male control that never throughout the course of their marriage did she have any awareness of what went on outside the four walls of her house, what work her husband did, let alone the state of his business. And therefore with his death – this man who reigned in everything, who had concentrated all power in his hands, who acknowledged no one's authority but his own, whose own wife and children, even, were strangers to him – with the death of this autocrat, all those men whom he had successfully used as tools in his hands, whom he had taught and trained and brought to perfection in stealing and trickery, those men now came to the fore and took over the situation.

The only friend the family had was Simon Hagorich. Following the agha's death, the field opened up for that old robber and former police bureaucrat. This man who had served as the agha's attorney now became Mrs. Masisian's main advisor.

One night, Mrs. Masisian, Gayané, and Hripsimé, all dressed in black, were sitting together in their room with him. The latter was sitting next to the lamp, his big spectacles resting on his enormous nose, and he was totally absorbed in looking at a piece of paper which he alternately brought close to his eyes, held at a distance and sometimes set on his knees to read. In this, he resembled an antiquarian who sat in silent concentration perusing some ancient page of faded text, trying to decipher the inscrutable hieroglyphics. The piece of paper was a telegram that Mrs. Masisian and her daughters were very anxious for Simon Hagorich to explain to them, for their happiness or grief was at stake in it.

The letter was just a few lines long, short and to the point: 'It's impossible for me to come. Mikayel will be coming instead. He'll take care of everything that needs to be taken care of.' It was signed, 'Stepan Masisian'.

This cool, brief, laconic message didn't sit well with Ms. Mariam; her motherly concerns weren't at all met by a few heartless sentences like this. 'It's impossible for me to come,' but why? What was wrong? These were the thoughts that began tormenting her. The only possibility she could think of was that Stepan was sick.

"Akh, what's happened?" she asked in a plaintive voice. "Stepan was a good boy, very good. It's not like him to leave me alone. Akh, dear God, what could it be?'

"My goodness, something must have happened to prevent him from coming," said Simon Hagorich, trying to comfort her.

Though Gayané and Hripsimé were sad about their brother, they were nevertheless secretly happy that they'd be able to see Mikayel again. In the course of the last few years they had heard so much about him that he had become something of a legendary figure to them.

But Simon Hagorich found the news extremely upsetting; he was hoping that if Stepan couldn't come, he himself would be designated the main executor of the agha's estate. He stood more to gain from dealing with an inexperienced and inept Stepan, than with a knowledgeable Mikayel whose 'devilishness' had long ago been evident to him. This old wolf had his mind set on making a big killing from the agha's estate, which all sorts of parties were trying to carve up for themselves. But now that plan was subverted. With the memory of the deceased in mind, he poured out his disapproval of Mikayel.

"May light be shed upon your soul, Bedros Agha," he declaimed, crossing himself. "You knew what Simon Hagorich was worth. You consulted him in everything; you had confidence in him and would say, 'Simon Hagorich, do whatever you think is best'. I'd take care of business for him, and within a few days' time I'd get all his money back. But now they don't even want to see my face, let alone pay me any attention . . . God knows what I've gone through to serve the interests of this household!"

"You're still with us, Simon Hagorich, and you'll still play the same role. Nothing will be done without your advice," said Mrs. Masisian reassuringly.

At that the old attorney assumed a very sincere manner and said with great feeling, "I swear to God, my heart is pained, my day has passed. I may die today or tomorrow. For me there's no difference between money and the cold earth. What can I take with me from this world of mine? My shroud is enough. . . . But look, it's for them that my heart hurts," he said pointing to the two girls. "It's them I want to help. Whatever happens to Stepan, he's a man and he'll make it, but they're just little girls . . ." Quite stunned at all this talk from the old trickster, Ms. Mariam heard him out without really understanding what he was trying to say.

"If the agha opened his eyes from the grave now and saw what's going on, his poor heart would burst with anger! My God, who's waiting to take over his estate? A mere baby who can't even tell black from white. Everyone knows who Simon Hagorich is. Twenty-two years I worked for the police and for fifteen with T. . . the governor, my hair's gone grey arguing suits and I know the Code as well as the Lord's Prayer, but no one knows what respect is anymore . . ." Quite confused by all this talk, Mrs. Masisian didn't really know what he was driving at, for like all calculating people Simon Hagorich never spoke plainly but always kept his true intentions under his hat.

"What are you trying to say, Simon Hagorich?" she asked, at last running out of patience.

Before answering, the old attorney took a pinch of snuff and drew it up his nostrils. Feeling better now, he coughed a couple of times and picked up Stepan's message again.

"I'll tell you, ma'am: Stepan says that in his place he's sending Mikayel to come and settle the agha's affairs. That has to mean he gave Mikayel a letter of authority, but he had no right to, not on behalf of you and your daughters. He speaks only for himself in a letter like that, that's all there is to it. Simon Hagorich will do his best to settle everything for you. All I need now is a similar letter from you and your daughters giving me authority, then we'll see how things work out. . ."

Ms. Mariam pondered a few moments then responded:

"We'll see . . . Just let Mikayel get here, then we'll think about it. . ."

"No ma'am, you don't understand. You'd better think about it good and hard," the old trickster interrupted gravely. "Out there in town your husband's store has been closed and sealed up while you sit here at home all safe and sound . . . Someone wants to get his hands on whatever's left, don't you understand?"

Sealing up the store until the heirs were determined was merely a legal formality and precaution on the part of the government, but from the way Simon Hagorich presented it to her the ill-informed widow was horrified and could only conclude that everything in it would end up in someone else's hands – while Simon Hagorich was that very man.

"What kind of letter do you need, Simon Hagorich?" she asked.

"Don't worry, I know exactly how it works," he answered proudly. "We'll go to the notary in the morning. I'll have the letter written up and everything will be taken care of."

"Then they'll unseal the store, right?"

"All the same day. Never underestimate Simon Hagorich!"

Mrs. Masisian agreed to give him whatever document was necessary to 'make sure her children had enough to eat', and at that Simon Hagorich stood up very satisfied with himself and prepared to leave.

"So I'll be here in the morning to take you to the notary," he said.

"Wait a minute, you haven't had a drink," said Mrs. Masisian.

"Well, yes, it would be nice to wet my whistle. Lord knows, my throat is parched from talking so much."

"Hripsimé, please bring some aragh for Simon Hagorich," said Mrs. Masisian. Hripsimé brought the aragh, and after having a good swig of his favorite beverage the old police drunkard left.

It was completely dark outside now and, as they say, one could hardly see one's hand in front of one's face. Emerging from the darkness some men who had been waiting for him in the street approached and fell into hushed conversation with Simon Hagorich:

"If the police get any wind of this it's over for us . . ."

"What if they betray us? . . ."

"It would be best if they sealed the secret back door as well as the others . . ."

"It's too late for that . . . Everything's gone, anyway . . ."

"Just get out of here and don't worry. I've taken care of everything," said Simon Hagorich to his interlocutors.

Following Simon Hagorich's departure Mrs. Masisian was visited by two neighbors, one an elderly woman and the other a quite attractive young lady. "Could you please tell me how the terrible event occurred?" the older woman asked after finishing with the usual condolences to the widow.

Mrs. Masisian had already told the remarkable story of her husband's death at least a hundred times and now had to tell it again, just to satisfy this neighbor's curiosity:

> It was the middle of the night. Gayané and Hrispimeh had gone to bed long ago and there wasn't any light in the agha's room. He was asleep, too. I was the only one who couldn't sleep. Something was bothering me – I myself didn't know what – and I couldn't calm down. The roosters had already been crowing for a good while. I was sitting next to the lamp darning the agha's socks when I suddenly heard a strange sound from his room, repeated several times. With my heart pounding I ran straight to his room. The poor man had got out of bed and fallen on the floor. He was in a frightful state. When he saw me, he got up from the floor and sat down. I was horrified when I saw his face; it was totally changed and

distorted. It was covered with a deathly color and his eyes were blazing terribly. 'My house is destroyed!' he shouted pitifully.

It was shocking. He kept beating his head and pulling his hair. I went up and took hold of his hands. 'What's wrong?' I asked him. I thought he had lost his mind; all his movements and words showed that he had lost control of himself. But after he had calmed down a bit he began repeating those same words again: 'Our home has been destroyed . . . We're done for . . .' Then he put his hands over his eyes and started crying.

'What's wrong, what's happened?' I asked him again.

'Well, what do you think? The golden rooster died!'

'How could that be?' I asked him.

'He died! I saw it with my own eyes.'

He said the golden rooster had appeared to him with his golden hen and chicks. They were walking around in the garden, flitting here and there and enjoying themselves. Suddenly two hoopoes[*] swooped down on them from the air. The poor hen and rooster fought long and hard to protect their chicks, but they couldn't. The hoopoes took them all in their claws and tore them limb from limb. Then they left them on the ground and disappeared into the sky.

'It sounds like a dream,' I said trying to comfort him.

'A dream. . . ? What do you mean, a dream. . . ? I saw it with my own eyes. . . Look! Look and see how bloody it is. . . The blood is still wet,' he said. He held out his hand as if to show me the last golden feather that was left of the rooster, but I didn't see anything. Just then he was gripped by some frightful disturbance again, and he fell into his tortured state. Then he relaxed a bit, little by little, but suddenly his entire body shuddered, his face became contorted, and he closed his eyes.

'Our home has been destroyed!' he cried out for the last time.

Then he went limp and fell to the floor. . .

Ms. Mariam's visitors were overwhelmed by her story. Gayané and Hripsimé were crying, and the guests also couldn't hide their tears.

"But what was that 'golden rooster'?" one of them asked.

"It was our home's good luck. All of our wealth came from it," answered Mrs. Masisian. She was just as superstitious as her late husband, and everyone in the household, except Stepan, believed in the beneficent power of the 'golden rooster.'

"That's true," affirmed one of the ladies. "Every home depends for its good luck on some particular creature, and when it disappears so does their good luck. I know they used to tell a story about a family in our town who had a snake living in their house. They said at night the snake would set cloves of garlic out in front of its nest. The family would gather them up, and the next morning they'd see that they had all turned into pure gold. Then one day a foolish member of the family got hold of one of the snake's babies and cut off its tail. The snake got angry and disappeared for good, and the family lost its gold and fell into poverty."

Thus, Mrs. Masisian and her guests talked long into the night as it slipped away imperceptibly. They then returned to the topic of the agha's ominous death.

"But what did the doctor say when he came and saw him?" one of the ladies asked.

"He said it was a stroke," answered Mrs. Masisian.

"Bah! What do they know about such things!" said one of her guests.

Chapter 7

Return and Reckoning

After an absence of more than five years Mikayel finally returned to the Masisian home. In those five years he had resided for the most part in Moscow, once a year attending the commercial fair at Nizhny Novgorod,* and several times traveling to Marseilles from which he visited many European cities.

His arrival caused the same sort of stir in the household as had been caused by his first arrival years before when he had ended up there straight from his village with all his peasant roughness. Everything he said then and every move he made became the object of laughter in the home. But now he returned from his experiences in European cities a totally transformed man, cultured and refined, his peasant roughness smoothed away. Now his every word and every move called forth respect and approval.

In those five years a great deal had changed in the Masisian home, as indeed Mikayel himself had changed. Ms. Mariam had aged a great deal beneath the burden of all her woes and cares. Gayané now resembled an old penitent nun in a convent; all she was missing was the worry beads and a black habit. But Hripsimé had developed, had grown more elegant and beautiful. Her stubborn childish willfulness had now given way to a tender, charming delicacy. She was now at that happy stage of life in which one becomes capable of loving and being loved.

Nothing had changed in the home; everything was just as it had always been before – except for one thing: the agha was no longer there.

A week had passed since Mikayel's return and for most of that week the family had hardly seen anything of him. His whole day was taken up dealing with the deceased agha's affairs. He left early in the morning and returned late at night all tired out, often in so bad a mood that it was impossible to say a word or spend a moment with him. The family had given him what used to be Stepan's room, and every time he returned home Mrs. Masisian would impatiently go in and ask him:

"What did you get done?"

"Nothing so far," Mikayel would usually answer.

The following is the long letter he wrote to Stepan one night:

"I found your father's business in as bad a state as I had feared. All the stores were empty. Anything of minimal value has been carted off. And do you know by whom? By your father's own henchmen. His sudden death gave those robbers the opportunity they were looking for, and the indifference of the local authorities made their job that much easier.

I don't blame anyone. Like your father often used to say, 'It's the smart one's who steal.' He saw stealing as one of the preconditions of life and therefore taught the men under him how to be perfect thieves, tested and true. But the poor man didn't understand that the weapons he was forging against others would some day be turned against himself with terrible force. . .

I've been confronted with a host of obstacles in straightening out the mess I found the business in. Everything is in such a tangled state and tied up in so many little knots that it's hardly possible to undo them. And the really disturbing part is that there are so many crimes involved that if they ever came to light many men would be well on their way to Siberia, which I think neither you nor I would want.

Imagine such dishonesty: Your father had a lawyer who worked for him (you never knew the worthless character), a man who had been 'in and out of every kind of little hole', as they say; a lackey type who had spent most of his life serving as a lowly errand boy for others, engaging in illicit practices from which an even fairly honest person couldn't help but learn all sorts of dishonest tricks. Acting as your father's lawyer, this man would rob the people who owed him money. After your father's death the man drove your innocent mother into such a state of desperation that he became her confidant and even the guardian over your young sisters. Thus did the flock come under the wolf's control. Then this crook and your father's former employees teamed up to commit all kinds of indescribable malfeasance against his property.

A few examples are sufficient to give you an idea what they did: all sorts of people showed up to claim supposed debts owed by your father, and the lawyer was prevailed upon to pay out sizable amounts to them. It's obvious to me that your father was never short of money and didn't borrow from anyone. But where did these creditors come from? All of that was fabricated by the employees themselves. All of them knew how to forge your father's signature. You know very well that your father was illiterate and that the only thing he wrote was his signature, which made forging it quite easy.

The false creditors appeared in court to make their claims, and your father's lawyer, who was also your sisters' guardian, backed up their claims.

As difficult as it might be to make an issue of this malfeasance, it would at the same time be quite easy to prove; but as I mentioned above there are so many crimes involved that the fate of many individuals is at stake. I will leave this for you to decide and await your instructions.

I still remember what you said to me in Moscow, 'What comes with the flood is taken away by the flood' . . . and that's just the way it has turned out. Your father had built his wealth on such a flimsy, rotten foundation that one couldn't have expected any other outcome; everything was bound to be lost and evaporate into thin air after he died. . . Your mother, who should have taken over affairs and protected what was left to her, doesn't know a thing about business. Out of her inexperience and ignorance she's delivered herself and your sisters right into the jaws of monsters. But how can she be blamed? It's understandable that all a woman's property will end up in a stranger's hands after her husband dies, for during his lifetime she was never accorded the status of a friend or partner and was shut away within the four walls of her house completely ignorant of what her husband did for a living. Your father sowed the seeds of his own destruction. . . If only he had kept some decent records, but everything is gone. . .'

He went on to describe the agha's death, his vision of the 'golden rooster' and the last golden feather that had remained in his hand from that guarantor of the family's good fortune and prosperity.

And taking that dream-like fantasy as an allegory for reality, Mikayel added:

"All that was left of that 'golden rooster' was a single feather in your father's hand. . . and thus, all that remains to his heirs of the wealth that the 'golden rooster' produced is just a little part. . . But, in reality, what was that 'golden rooster' that oversaw your family's prosperity and through its beneficial influence made it possible for your father's enterprises to succeed? Nothing but the invisible personification of your father's trickery, cunning, deviousness, unscrupulousness and other such unethical traits. . . He died, this skillful operator, and with him died the 'golden rooster'. . . The superstitious can believe what they will, but this is how I see the meaning of that ancient tradition in your family."

At the end of the letter Mikayel gave Stepan the latest news about his mother and sisters and went on at length about what a beautiful and graceful girl Hripsimé had become, etc.

Mrs. Masisian entered with a sad expression and sat down beside him just as he was sealing the letter.

"Did you write to Stepan and tell him to come home quickly?" she asked.

"He doesn't need me to tell him that. He'll come home when his work is done," answered Mikayel.

"Akh, but what's going to become of us by the time he comes back!"

"I think everything will be just fine. Stepan himself is a great treasure for you. You're lucky to have a son like him. What else do you want?"

"I believe what you say," she said somewhat comforted. "But I wouldn't mind being poor and not having enough to eat if only he could be here. I'm afraid I'll die without seeing him. . ."

"You'll see him and soon enough, ma'am. He won't abandon you."

"What did you write about us?" Mrs. Masisian asked.

"A lot of things. . . I told him everything. . ."

"Did you tell him that 'the golden rooster' died?"

"I did. . ."

"Akh, what a tragedy that was!" she said with a great sigh and dabbed her eyes with a handkerchief.

"But Stepan will bring you a new kind of good fortune; he'll create a new 'golden rooster' for you, better than the old one," said Mikayel.

Mrs. Masisian left the room feeling better.

Gayané and Hripsimé hadn't been able to spend a moment with Mikayel from the day he arrived. They'd only see him from a distance, and as soon as he appeared they would run off to their room. Mikayel wasn't surprised at this odd behavior, for he was long familiar with it as the norm in this province. He and the two girls, who had lived under the same roof and grown up together for so many years, were now practically strangers and acted like they didn't know each other. This wasn't due only to the passage of the few years they hadn't seen each other, but rather to the fact that all of them had developed to a new stage of life. Mikayel had grown up and become a man and the two girls were of an age at which it was improper for them to be left alone with a man. This is why their mother warned them the first day Mikayel arrived:

"You know, even though Mikayel is taking your brother's place here, you're big girls now and its not right for you to be talking to a grown man."

The two sisters initially went along with their mother's counsel, but in time a growing strain of protest began to surface in their conversations.

"You know what, Gayané? Today when Mikayel came home I was near the front door and when he knocked I opened it. He smiled and said hello to me, but I didn't say anything. He just put his head down, passed by me and went to his room. Afterwards I felt so terribly ashamed of myself. Akh, what does he think of me now. He'll probably think, what a completely stupid girl!"

"No he won't. He's very familiar with our customs here," said Gayané.

"What customs!" said Hripsimé somewhat heatedly. "Is Mikayel a stranger that we shouldn't say a word to him?"

"No, sis, he's not a stranger, but what would others say?"

"What could they say? Is it any of their business if we talk to a man who's part of our household?"

Gayané assumed a more advisory tone now, seeing how upset her sister was:

"That's true, but don't you know the walls have ears? And if word gets out, everyone will know."

"So? Let them know! Who cares?"

"Then our name will be sullied and people will talk all kinds of evil about us."

"But it's clear that Mikayel is like our brother."

"Yes, but he had a different father."

"To be honest, Gayané, I really want to talk with Mikayel. Haven't you noticed what a fine man he's turned into?"

"I've noticed. . ." Gayané answered darkly.

"I don't think he has an equal in our entire town."

"No, he doesn't. . ."

Their mother entered and the sisters put an end to their conversation.

Chapter 8

An Outing in the Country

Winter passed, spring passed, six months had passed since the agha died. It was Sunday. This was a very significant day for the Masisians, for it was the day they were to come out of mourning and put away their black clothing to dress normally again. The significance for Mikayel was that Gayané and Hripsimé would for the first time wear the dresses he had brought for them from Moscow.

A group of ladies arrived early in the morning to carry out the appropriate rites. They changed Mrs. Masisian's and the girls' clothing from black into white, then led them to church. After church they all went to the graveyard where the ceremony for the repose of souls was conducted. Then they all went to the Masisian's farm to have lunch together. Gayané and Hripsimé looked stunning in their new dresses. Mikayel was the only man there but kept his distance from the group of ladies.

Having arrived at the farm the guests gathered under a shelter woven out of branches and shaded by the enormous limbs of an apricot tree. Mrs. Masisian set about preparing the meal with the help of some of the older women, while the girls and younger women went off to take a walk around the farm, taste the fruit and pass the time until lunch was ready. But Gayané, Hripsimé and a group of friends broke away from the others and went off in their own direction.

It didn't take long for Mikayel to start feeling uncomfortable at the gathering. Only the older women would get anywhere near him. The young girls avoided him because it was considered improper for young girls to have anything to do with him. He took a walk to a remote portion of the farm and there encountered the old caretaker.

"Hello Khacho."

"Why hello, son. God bless you."

"There doesn't seem to be much fruit on the trees this year."

"No, that's right, and there aren't many grapes either.

"But why?"

"Only God knows. . . But the way it looks to me, this farm was cursed the day Bedros agha died. You should have seen it before, it was a real paradise. The trees were so loaded with fruit we had to prop up the branches, and there was no end of grapes. Everyone that came by wandered around, took and ate what they wanted, and still we had enough left to fill more than a hundred barrels of wine every year; but now. . ."

"I have a feeling you didn't dig up the soil around the trees enough. And look at the vines, they're all overgrown with weeds."

"No, agha, that's not it."

"Then what?"

"Didn't you hear about the tragedy."

"What tragedy?"

"The Golden Rooster died. . ."

"I know. . ."

"So, don't you see, that's why. When it died everything went wrong here – no fruit, no grapes. . . . Between the hail and the caterpillars everything was ruined."

Mikayel had no response, and Khacho went on:

"I've worked on this farm for over twenty years. I took care of all the trees like my own children. Look, with these hands I pruned them and brought them to maturity," he said, showing Mikayel his calloused hands. "But now I tell you my heart is broken, nothing seems right, especially since I heard. . ."

"Heard what?"

"That the farm is going to be sold off to pay Bedros Agha's debts. As soon as I heard it I felt like someone had stuck a knife in my heart. Who's ever heard of such a thing! Bedros Agha's wealth could've damned up the Arax river he had so much. What could've happened to it all that they have to come now and sell off the farm?"

"Don't you worry, Khacho, it won't be sold."

"Akh, I'd die if they sold it!" Khacho said as he wiped some tears away from his eyes.

Khacho had every reason to be sad, for a lien had already been placed on the farm. But through his diligence and hard work Mikayel had been able to postpone the date of sale for several months.

Mikayel was no less troubled about the matter than the old farm keeper. After offering him his final words of comfort, he left.

Nevertheless an atmosphere of delightful tranquility reigned in the farm. Not a leaf was stirring in the stillness. The blazing sun was pouring down mightily on the solid green canopy of the trees, but on the ground beneath the trees the air was cool and fresh. Ensconced here song birds flitted from branch to branch, their sweet piping echoing in the pristine stillness. But Mikayel was entirely immune to nature's bewitching loveliness. He wandered gloomily through the forest like a lost soul, his thoughtless gaze fixed before him on the high walls of hedges bordering the path on either side.

In the distance he saw the group of girls running and circling about like wood nymphs, enjoying themselves beneath the trees. He withdrew to the side of the path to hide from them. Two girls out of this happy group detached themselves from the others and came in his direction, searching for patches of three-leafed clover hidden in the grass and trying to find a four-leafed one among them. One of the girls was Hripsimé and the other a girl he didn't know.

"Why do you keep on looking?" Hripsimé's friend asked.

"Oh, I just have to find one!" said Hripsimé, still rustling delicately through the grass with her fingers.

"Goodness, what good would it do if you found one?"

"To see what my fortune will be."

"You've already got what you want, what else could you be looking for?" said Hripsimé's friend with a sarcastic smile.

"No, that's a lie Nazani," said Hripsimé blushing.

"What do you mean, a lie, when the whole town is talking about it?"

"What are they saying?"

"They say the servant boy in your house – what's his name? Oh yes, Mikayel – is in love with you."

"I swear, Nazani, I don't know what they're talking about."

"Well, do you love him though?"

"I. . ."

But Mikayel did not hear what 'I' answered, as the girls had already passed him by. Nevertheless, the little he had overheard was unforgettable. Since the agha died Mikayel had been so engrossed in caring for the poor family he had left behind that he didn't have a moment to commune with his own heart and soul, let alone show any interest in Hripsimé whom he had never looked on 'with a suitor's eye', as they say. But today he saw her as he must have, for today she had been revealed to him in all her captivating beauty and he had found her incomparably bewitching.

It was well past noon and time to eat. All the girls and women came back from various directions and gathered at the shelter. Though dinner was ready, Mikayel was still waiting for two acquaintances who had promised to come to the farm and dine with him, two officials who worked for the tribunal. They finally arrived and Mikayel went over to greet them.

"It seems we're a bit late," one of them said as he shook Mikayel's hand.

"Not very, the ladies just sat down to eat," said Mikayel.

"Oh my, quite a large group. Bah! Weren't we supposed to eat with them?" said one of the men.

"A nice idea, but I'm afraid they'd never allow it," said Mikayel.

"But frankly, isn't it ridiculous for us eat by ourselves?" asked the man.

"I don't think we'd enjoy their company that much. After all, what can you talk about with them? You won't understand them and they won't understand you. Then all you can do is sit there with your mouth shut and just look at them. Besides, we'd just spoil their fun."

So saying, Mikayel led his guests to a table specially prepared for them in the shade of a large pear tree, and old Khacho the farm keeper served as their waiter.

The men's conversation was mostly taken up with Masisian's death, the 'golden rooster', and the misdeeds of Simon Hagorich and Masisian's employees, all of which were the talk of the town by now.

"You know what, Mikayel, they've already arrested four of Masisian's men and they're in jail now."

"It's too late," said Mikayel coldly. "That's just playing music after the wedding's over. Locking them up now is useless. Most of the property is gone already."

"But they'll be sent to Siberia."

"What good does that do? It won't help feed Masisian's family, that's for sure."

"I'm really astonished. I couldn't ever have imagined such criminality."

"The astonishing thing is that they kept their jobs as long as they did," responded Mikayel bitterly. "What galls me the most isn't just all the stock they stole but that boxful of IOU's. They took them and sold them back to the agha's debtors for next to nothing. Not only that, they forged a bunch of false ones under his name and sold them to all kinds of shysters to use. It's all very complex, but if a decent investigation were done all kinds of people would be implicated, even some no one would ever have suspected."

"But what did those crooks do with all that money?"

"You must have heard the saying, 'When one thief stole from another, God looked on and was amazed'. The money went to other crooks like themselves who gave them protection . . . With the destruction of Masisian's house, ten or twenty houses were built . . ."

"Then his family will be left in poverty."

"I'm not sure yet . . ." was all Mikayel could say.

After dinner Mikayel's guests wanted to go swimming in the river that bordered the farm. Though he wasn't at all interested in swimming, he walked along with them toward the river. The ladies, as well, had finished their meal and set off to take walks in the farm.

When Mikayel and his friends arrived at the river he parted company with them and found a shady spot under a walnut tree. He stretched out on the grass and fell into a deep meditative state listening to the sound of the river and observing how its currents billowed and frothed and struck violently against the trees along the bank before flowing on.

Looking down on this river Mikayel was reminded of the Arax near which he had spent the most precious days of his childhood and his friends there, those dear, good-hearted pals with whom he had been so happy. He remembered his grandma Shushan and Uncle Aved, both of whom were now in their graves . . . And those days of childhood came and went before his mind's eye like a dream, like the impetuous flow of the river that bespoke a turbulent life . . .

This part of the farm came to an abrupt end at the river's edge, and at certain points the trees grew right down to its banks. Suddenly the pervasive clamor of the river was piercd by a tremendous cry of distress. Mikayel jumped to his feet and ran toward the sound. Some panic-stricken girls were immersed deep in thickets . . . Hripsimé was on the ground, trapped in the clutches of an enormous raging dog . . . Mikayel grabbed one of the poles used to support some vines and made swift work of the dog with three blows to its head. It collapsed to the ground and lay there motionless.

Hripsimé had a small wound on her arm and a blood stain on the sleeve of her summer dress, but she wasn't critically injured. Neverteless, Mikayel knew how dangerous a dog bite could be and immediately swept her up in his arms and carried her back to her mother who was extremely shaken on finding out what had happened to her daughter. Under the shock of what had happened all the ladies and girls left the farm immediately to return to their homes, while Hripsimé was placed on a horse and sent back into town.

Chapter 9

Two and Two Together

The doctor verified that the bite and scratches the dog had inflicted on Hripsimé weren't grave. A week later she was on her feet again, though still weak and pale. Her arm was healed, but Cupid's arrow had opened a new wound in her heart and a sort of errant fire burned in her eyes.

Until that day Hripsimé's heart had been invulnerable, but now certain dark, ill-defined feelings began to torment her, something she couldn't understand. She became sad and withdrawn and avoided company. In her solitude her lovely black eyes would suddenly fill with unexpected tears.

Mrs. Masisian couldn't help but notice the sudden change in her behavior. "What's wrong with you, girl?" she would ask. "Oh, nothing . . ." she would answer.

Given the intimacy that exists between sisters, they often open up their hearts to each other; and thus Gayané tried to draw the truth out of her sister that her mother had been powerless to do:

"What's going on, Hripsimé? You've gone as pale as an autumn leaf," she asked as they sat in the garden one day.

"I don't know myself, sis," said Hripsimé, looking down.

"No, there's something going on that you don't want to tell me about, but I know . . ."

Hripsimé didn't say a word. She kept her head down and played her fingers through the grass, struggling to relieve her anxiety . . .

"You think if you don't tell me I won't know," said Gayané playfully.

"About what?"

"Why you're so sad."

"I don't want to hear about it, not a word!" said Hripsimé, standing up to leave.

"Stay here for a minute, sit down," said Gayané, taking hold of Hripsimés arm.

Hripsimé sat back down and Gayané continued:

"Why be embarassed, Hripsimé? Just be frank with me. I know you're in love . . ."

Hripsimé said nothing, but she blushed slightly and the glow in her lovely eyes spoke volumes. Gayané hugged her and gave her a kiss. Hripsimé gave in and started to cry softly. In a while she felt better and was ready to talk:

"I swear, sis, I don't really know if I'm in love or not. I haven't had any peace of mind since that dog attacked me. Whether I'm awake or asleep, I always see him . . . I'm always talking to him . . ."

"But not when you're awake," observed Gayané with a smile.

"I do, in my mind . . ." Hripsimé answered, "When I see him I want to say something, but I freeze up. I don't know what to say . . . It seems like he avoids me and I feel really terrible about it. Have you noticed how late he's been coming home? When he gets back he immediately disappears into his room, and in the morning he's gone again before you ever see him . . ."

The two of them sat in the garden talking about Mikayel until the evening slowly turned to night, one of those cool and tranquil summer nights that are so refreshing after a stifling day. But as they sat there talking they didn't know that someone was hidden nearby listening to every word they said.

"Let's go back inside," said Gayané, standing up to return to the house. But Hripsimé was still too agitated to go back in.

"It's still early, let's take a little walk," she said nervously.

The moonlight now penetrated the leafy canopy and dappled the garden paths before them. The eavesdropper now silently stole out of the garden and went directly to Mrs. Masisian's room. This was Nuné, the daughter who had for years been banished from the family. She had recently returned home on two important occasions: once for her father's funeral, and once when Hripsimé was sick.

Nuné found her mother alone inside. The lamp light falling on her straight, well-formed figure revealed a comely picture. What a remarkable similarity there was between her and Hripsimé, for Hripsimé was the very copy of that somewhat aged and worn original, though fresher and gayer than her oldest sister.

Nuné told her mother about the conversation she had overheard in the garden.

"I already knew about it, but what can we do?" said Ms. Mariam.

Nuné drew closer to her mother and dropped her voice:

"It's clear that Hripsimé's in love, but now it's time to find out if Mikayel feels the same way."

"How can we do that? He's extremely private. It's hard to get anything out of him."

"You can't hide love, it'll come out on it's own. Listen Mama, we have to do something to help bring things to a head . . ."

In the course of a few brief moments Ms. Mariam's face had registered the rapid alternations of joy and sadness she was going through, and her heart was shuddering like a leaf in the wind.

"Is it really possible to bring things to a head?" she said incredulously. "Frankly, Nuné, I'm all confused and I really don't know what to do . . . May the Lord grant Hripsimé her heart's desire or else who knows what will become of her?"

"Don't worry Mama, they'll find a way themselves," said Nuné calmly. "We just have to give them the space to show their feelings, then 'the water will find its own path.'"

"But it's hard, so hard," Ms. Mariam answered, still incredulous. "Right now people are fighting over Mikayel, offering him their daughters from every side – and girls from really wealthy families, too, with huge doweries. And what do we have to offer? It would be different if your father were still alive and we had what we used to have . . ." the poor woman said, as large tears began to roll down her cheeks.

"I don't think Mikayel's after money. To him Hripsimé is the treasure," said Nuné reassuringly.

"Ah, darling, everybody wants money. Don't you see how no one pays us any attention anymore? But before . . . before! They used to feel honored if we spoke to them or even gave them a glance . . ."

"That's true Mama, but I still don't believe that Mikayel is a man to be fooled by money. From what I've heard, he has quite a bit himself."

"But a little more wouldn't hurt, would it? Who ever gets enough?"

"Nevertheless, I have faith that things will work out. We shouldn't despair," said Nuné.

"We'll see . . . We'll see what God allows . . ." said Ms. Mariam.

Just then Gayané and Hripsimé burst into the room with beaming faces and put an end to the conversation.

Meanwhile Mikayel was alone in his room. He picked a letter up from the table to read it again. It was Stepan's reply to his letter of a few months earlier in which he had reported to Stepan all the details surrounding his father's death and how his wealth had been stolen.

"Everything in this letter reflects his depth of character. He's the same frank, wise person as always," said Mikayel to himself. The letter read as follows:

> Being a doctor, I looked at my father's wealth from a purely medical point of view. If a patient has an abscess, then I either wait for it to burst and heal on its own, or I lance it. One can always expect a concentration of filth in the body to lead to trouble. My father's wealth was a gigantic abscess, and even though his assistants were crooked they performed a vital role by lancing and draining it . . . The patient couldn't withstand the pain and died, but his heirs recovered . . .

Then a few lines later he went on to talk about his father's employees.

> For the love of God, let those pathetic men be. They're not to blame. After all, who taught them to steal? They were simply my father's loyal disciples and they practiced the lessons he taught them to perfection. No, I feel sorry for them, so give them a break.

Suddenly the doors to Mikayel's room opened and in came Hripsimé.

"What is it, Hripsimé?" asked Mikayel.

"Dinner's ready and my mother's asking for the pleasure of your company," Hripsimé answered in a faltering voice.

"Oh, you're so polite, Hripsimé! Where did you learn to talk like that?" said Mikayel standing up and taking her hands into his.

Hripsimé couldn't find the words to respond but only blushed.

"But seriously, Hripsimé, I have to caution you again. You haven't been taking very good care of yourself. You're still not fully recovered and you could have a relapse if you go for walks in the garden like you did this evening. It's really damp, especially after the last rain."

Looking Mikayel straight in the face, Hripsimé asked, "You saw me walking in the garden?"

"Yes, I saw you. You and Gayané were sitting together, then you got up to take a walk."

"Then you must have heard what we were talking about," she said with a slight smile.

"I didn't hear a thing. I don't make it a practice to listen in on young girls' conversations. Nuné's the one who does that sort of thing."

"Really?" said Hripsimé sharply. "Then she must have heard what we were talking about. Oh, what a devil!"

At this remark Mikayel suddenly put two and two together: As he was taking a walk in the garden earlier in the evening he had noticed Nuné hiding in the trees eavesdropping on the conversation between Gayané and Hripsimé and suspected that she must have had a serious reason for doing so. Now seeing Hripsimé blush and act so flustered, his suspicion was confirmed.

"So you see, I know everything," he said, looking her straight in the eyes.

"No you don't, you just want to get me to talk," she said with a laugh.

"Why would I do that?"

"So you can find out what we were talking about . . . But I won't tell you no matter how hard you try. . ."

"Maybe you won't, but Gayané will, because she's nice."

"So – does that mean I'm bad?"

"No, but you're stubborn."

"Of course, of course, but now let's go, they're waiting for us," she said taking hold of Mikayel's hand and practically dragging him out of the room.

Hripsimé was no longer the withdrawn, anxiety ridden person she had been a few weeks earlier, but the playful girl who had dumped water all over Mikayel on Vartavar years before. And now the Mikayel she saw before her was a well-dressed, highly cultured gentleman whose every gesture bespoke refinement and decency. He accepted her invitation and the two of them went together to Ms. Mariam's room to join the rest of the family for dinner. Relations between Mikayel and the family underwent a complete transformation after the incident at the farm and Mikayel now enjoyed the full freedom of a family member. "Now I have two sons: one is you, and the other is Stepan," Mrs. Masisian confided in him one day. Her three daughters often visited him in his room now and fell into conversation with him on a variety of subjects while straightening things up for him. They all took lunch and dinner together and sometimes tea in the morning if Mikayel wasn't detained in his room with important business. Evening strolls and conversation in the garden with the sisters had become the norm, with Mikayel doing most of the talking, usually describing his experiences in Europe and Moscow. But on this particular evening he chose to let them know as much as he could about Stepan's last letter.

Chapter 10

The Water Finds Its Way

Though the Masisians had lost their family fortune almost overnight and gone through a world of grief, they managed better than might have been expected. Life went on and they had everything they needed. The biggest difference now was the new sense of vibrancy and peace in their life.

The agha's fortune had always been just a vague abstraction to them, like the 'golden rooster' itself; only some distant feature of the marketplace, one whose benefits had never touched the core of a family life forever deprived even of the simplest joys. It was therefore only natural that they felt no particular pain on its disappearance.

A still greater source of comfort to the family lay in Mikayel's sweetness and selflessness. His warmth and solicitude made up for a multitude of evils and helped them set their troubles aside.

A family experiences deep happiness – like the warmth and radiant joy that follows a frightful storm – when a tyrannical order finally collapses and is replaced by love and unity and freedom. With the warmth and light of life that Mikayel brought into their midst the Masisians, who had never known one happy day in all their years, now found themselves in a completely new world. Only now did they begin to savor the delights of social contact – this family whose mother had been cut off from all contact with the outside world and was denied the right to talk to men even inside its walls. Only now did it become clear to them that happiness and prosperity don't depend only on the accumulation of money – money which, even if saved up into huge amounts, is subject to decay and if kept without being used turns into a poison. Only now could this family see that there was something else the absence of which would turn a home into a hell, as theirs had been: through Mikayel they received the vivifying power of love as their hell was transformed into a paradise.

The summer went by and winter arrived. Those two seasons with their opposite natures exercise a corresponding influence on people's lives: The heat of summer disperses people, but the cold of winter brings them together and makes social life more cohesive. The same is true in the life of a family, too, and Ms. Mariam's room now turned into a parlor. It came alive with light-hearted conversation as she, her daughters, Mikayel and occasional visitors gathered there to spend time together.

Nuné now lived with her mother and sisters again and sent for her two children, little Narkis and Rosdom, to come and join her from the village, as well as Brother Aved's two children who were Mikayel's first cousins. Brother Aved had died long ago and his widow had married another villager in keeping with village custom. Mikayel took the children in and cared for them, just as his uncle had done for him when he was an orphan. It had been many, many years since there were children in the Masisian home, but now it came to life again with their merry, innocent banter.

Only one person was missing to complete the family's happiness and that was Stepan. His letters indicated that he had to stay abroad for the time being and couldn't return home.

The ruined remains of Masisian's business were stabilized as much as could be hoped. Mikayel didn't bother pursuing what had already been plundered and lost . . . "You'll never bring the dead back from the grave," he would say. He felt that the best thing to do was to invest his energies in business rather that pursuing time consuming and fruitless suits. His main purpose was to protect the family from the most fraudulent of the claimants and hang onto the house, the farm, and some of the fixed property. This he was able to do partly by proving the invalidity of their claims and partly by paying them off. Of the agha's remaining property, Mikayel still had control of the money from the Moscow business. This, together with selling off some of the fixed property, provided just enough money for the family to live securely and comfortably.

Meanwhile Mikayel had completely set aside any thought for himself and placed the family's welfare ahead of his own. He worked for them as a man possessed, so totally identified with their fate that he never even considered any other course. In this he was responding to a sense of sacred obligation, for he had been raised in this household, had breathed its air, had been nourished by its care – though that bit of sustenance had come at the price of so much torment. But his tormentor was now gone. The rest of the family had always been kind and loving toward him, and now their love for him burst into flames and wiped away his somber past . . .

But there was also something else that bound Mikayel to this home: He had lately become acutely aware that he was in love with Hripsimé and felt he couldn't live happily without her. He noticed little signs that she felt the same way, but he had never broached the subject. There had been only vague references, meaningful smiles, movements of the eyebrows, exchanges of looks – the wordless ways in which Armenian girls find it easiest to express their feelings. Though quite urbane and sophisticated now, Mikayel was still reluctant to break provincial mores by adopting a direct course. For her part, Hripsimé knew that sooner or later he would have to raise the topic with her mother.

Hripsimé came to Mikayel's room one morning, her cheeks flushed from the cold outside.

"I came for your shirts. You said there were some buttons missing and I can sew them on for you now," she said standing at the door.

"Goodness, how impolite you are, Hripsimé!" said Mikayel walking up to her. "When you say good morning you're supposed to come up, take the person's hand and ask how they are. Then you're supposed to have a nice little conversation and share a laugh. Only then do you mention why you came."

"I don't know anything about those things. I just came for your shirts," said Hripsimé blushing heavily.

"I was just joking, Hripsimé. Your way is best – simple and clear. I love simplicity," said Mikayel taking hold of her hands. "But what a worrywort you are! I mentioned my buttons yesterday evening. I thought you would have forgotten about them by now."

"I'm not forgetful . . ."

Mikayel brought his shirts out and handed them to her.

"I'd like you to work on them here."

"Why, so you can make sure I do it right?"

"Not at all! I'd just like to watch you work."

Without saying anything Hripsimé took the shirts and sat down with them near the window.

"But don't distract me," she said as she began working on them.

"I won't. I'd just like to share a couple of things with you so you don't get bored," said Mikayel.

"More travel stories, I suppose."

"Wouldn't you like that?"

"Yes, but . . ."

"But what?"

"I'm not that interested."

"Then what? Shall I tell you a tale?"

"Tales are for old ladies."

"Then let me tell you about how girls and boys get along in Europe."

"I'll listen then!"

"European girls aren't shy around men like girls here. They let them know just how they feel. They talk to any man they want to; they take walks and go to dances with men and have all kinds of fun with them."

"But don't their mothers object?" said Hripsimé, interrupting him.

"No, because they know their daughters are sensible. They encourage them to learn all they can about their boyfriends so they're sure of their character. That's the only way they'll find the right husband. If the man measures up, the girl will begin to show her love. Otherwise, a girl could end up very unhappy, because marriage is a heavy yoke."

"Then don't the men test the girls the same way?"

"Of course."

"That's good . . ."

"I've told my story, Hripsimé; now you tell me how girls here go about choosing their husbands."

"You know very well . . ."

"But I've forgotten. I don't really remember that well."

"Girls here aren't allowed to be around boys. If a girl loves a boy she has to keep it to herself and can't tell anyone, not even the boy."

"Like you . . ." said Mikayel, taking Hripsimé's trembling hands in his.

She said nothing, but big tears formed in her eyes.

"Take me! Take me where the girls are free!" she said struggling to hold her feelings in check.

"I'll take you when you're my wife, Hripsimé," said Mikayel, somewhat losing his composure. "Well . . . Do you agree?"

"Yes," said Hripsimé softly.

Mikayel was about to kiss her, but she left the shirts where they were and ran out of the room. Mikayel stood petrified for several moments, then came to his senses. "What a pathetic girl!" he finally said to himself. "She's reserved to the bitter end; unless a priest has pronounced her lawfully married she regards a little hug or kiss as a sin."

That evening, right after sunset when it was starting to get cold outside, Mikayel had shut himself up in his room and sat anxiously tugging the hairs of his new grown moustache into his mouth, chewing on them as if they were a barrier to his speaking and expressing his heartache. At the opposite side of the room Nuné was trying to adjust the damp, poorly burning wood in the fireplace, which was sputtering and emitting a sort of melancholy whistle.

"The fire is sighing . . . That's a bad sign . . ." said Nuné superstitiously.

"Why do you say that?" asked Mikayel, seeming to wake up from his worries.

"I don't know, that's what they say. When a fire makes a sad sound they say it's crying," she said.

"Any living matter will make sad noises like that when it burns," observed Mikayel.

"Like your heart," said Nuné with a meaningful smile.

"Like Hripsimé's heart, too . . ." said Mikayel.

"But tell me now, what did you argue about with my mother," Nuné asked, coming to sit near Mikayel.

"It wasn't an argument, just a heated discussion. Did I insult anyone?"

"No, but it seems there were some hurt feelings . . ."

"Frankly Nuné, could anyone really be that old-fashioned? I went and saw your mother to declare my love for Hripsimé. I kissed her hand and asked for her blessing. She kissed my forehead and gave her blessing. But then we started talking about the details, and she said the wedding would have to wait a year until the mourning period for your father was over, otherwise there would be gossip. That was the substance of it."

"But what's your hurry?"

"You're just like your mother, Nuné. You just don't understand the situation I'm in. I have to get back to Moscow. If I stay here much longer I'll lose all my business, don't you understand? Besides, Hripsimé has to go with me so she can see the world and have new experiences. She's a fine, intelligent girl, but she still has a few things to learn . . . ."

"Why didn't you explain that to my mother?"

"I did, but she just keeps harping on the same point: 'I'll die of a broken heart if you take my daughter away' and so on. I don't know . . . What if we marry and I have to leave her here to go and live in another country? That's what most Armenian merchants do. I need to know how she feels about it, but I haven't seen her all day."

"She hasn't been acting herself lately. She wanders around all day like she's lost, crying to herself," said Nuné.

"The poor girl!" said Mikayel.

Mikayel's remark seemed to rekindle old wounds in Nuné's heart and she responded sharply:

"Well, my dear, that's the misery narrow-minded parents can cause for their children. There seems to be a curse on our family that keeps us from being happy. My oldest sister hanged herself. She was so good, so pretty, but her story's too awful to tell . . . And you know what happened to me. What did I do to be branded a bad woman?

My mother's good too, but what can you do with her? She only goes by what she's seen and heard."

Poor Nuné . . . . She'd been victimized her whole life by ignorant preconceptions, very personally bearing their full brunt. But when she had finished pouring out all her heartache, she paused and looked at Mikayel for a moment.

"Don't worry about anything, my dear. I'll have a talk with my mother and everything will work out. We've all been so unhappy, my sisters and I; let Hripsimé at least find some joy in life."

The marriage took place a week later in one of the churches in town with a small group of friends in attendance. Hripsimé and Mikayel stood with radiant faces before the altar. After the ceremony their friends came up one by one to congratulate them, and then they all got into the carriages waiting outside and went to the Masisian home to celebrate.

That night Mikayel received the following telegram from Stepan:

"My congratulations on your happiness. My father's destroyed home has come to life again, thanks to you. From now on you will be my family's true 'golden rooster'. . ."

ENDNOTES

Agha – A title of respect for a distinguished man in the community.

Agouletsi – A person from Agoulis, an ancient Armenian city located in what is the present-day region of Nakhichevan, Azerbaijan.

Aragh [also Raki, Oghi] – a colorless anise flavored brandy.

Arevdur – Literally, "take and give"; the Armenian word for trade.

Argus-eyed – In Greek mythology, Argus was the hundred-eyed giant who guarded the maiden Io.

Ashdarak – A town about 20 miles northwest of Yerevan.

Bench – Tacht (Arm.)

Bourse – The central commercial exchange building of a city.

Catherine – Empress Catherine the Great of Russia, 1762-96.

Charchi – Middleman.

Clover – [Raffi's note] A plant used in divination.

Cookhouse – Tonradoun (Armenian).

Dolma – stuffed vegetables

Emissaries – The mission referred to is of great historic importance.

In March of 1878, following the end of the Russo-Turkish War, the Armenian Patriarch of Constantinople dispatched three distinguished emissaries to meet with key European heads of state as well as attend the Berlin Conference to advocate for Armenian autonomy within the Ottoman Empire.

Faustus, Dr. – The central character from Christopher Marlow's drama *The Tragical History of Dr. Faustus*, in which the sorcerer Dr. Faustus promises his soul to satan in exchange for unlimited wordly power and pleasure.

Gharabagh [also, Karabagh, Artsakh] – an Armenian region north of Agoulis and southeast of Lake Sevan.

Gymnasium – In the European educational system, an academic high school that prepares students for university study.

Hoopoe – A bird with a long curved bill, broad crest and flamboyant markings.

Jan – A term of deep affection, similar to but stronger than 'dear'.

Jan-Gyouloum (O Precious Rose; fr. Persian and Turkish] – A divination song and dance in Armenia. It involves mostly girls who dance and sing as they circle around a girl standing in the center holding a container of flowers the girls have previously gathered from nature. The girls from the dancing circle go in turns to pick a flower from the bunch in order to see what their fortunes will be.

Kaloust – This name means "Advent" in Armenian.

Kedir – [Raffi's note] The *kedir* is like a large wooden box; a portable cabin mounted on four long poles and placed either in gardens or on rooftops to sleep in during the summer. It affords cool air and protection from poisonous insects.

Khoja – One of a distinctive class of Persian-Armenian merchants of the 18th century.

Knucklebones – A game similar to jacks.

Kopeck – One-hundredth of a rouble.

Kufteh – Stuffed meatballs.

Lake Kegham – Lake Sevan.

Lezgistan – The north Caucasian homeland of the Lezgi people in southern Russia near the Caspian Sea.

Manet – A regional denomination of money equivalent to one rouble.

Medlar – A small fruit tree of the rose family found in Europe and Asia Minor.

Nerses – Catholicos Nerses I the Great (353-372 AD), great-great grandson of Gregory the Illuminator. He led the struggle against paganism and established schools, orphanages, hospitals and refuge communities for the poor.

Nizhny Novgorod – The trade capital of Imperial Russia, about 600 miles east of Moscow, known as 'Gorki' in the Soviet era.

Refugees [Alashgertsi] – The approximately three thousand Armenian refugees driven from their homes in Alashgert into eastern Armenian as a result of the Russo-Turkish War (1877-78). They followed the retreating Russian Army into the region of Yerevan and there suffered great disease and hardship.

Rest [winter rest] – The reference is to the practice of keeping livestock locked up in winter refuges, often subterranean, to protect them from the elements and allow them to rest and fatten up for springtime.

Rouble – The basic Russian monetary denomination consisting of one hundred kopecks; roughly equivalent to half a dollar.

School – Raffi here uses the word *eskol* as a word foreign to the boys.

Shalvar – The traditional baggy trousers worn in the region.

Vartan – Vartan The Great, commander of the Armenian army in the battle of Avarayr in AD 451 in which Armenia fought against the Persian Empire to defend its autonomy as a Christian state.

Vartavar – A very popular religious feast in the middle of August originating in pagan Armenia but associated in the Christian era with The Transfiguration. The image of the rose is central to this festivity, and it is typically celebrated by children suddenly dumping water on people in public.

Zok – Nickname for a person from Agoulis.

RAFFI

ARMENIA'S FOREMOST NOVELIST

Authentic, first rate translations into English
*www.gomidas.org * info@gomidas.org*

www.ingramcontent.com/pod-product-compliance
Lightning Source LLC
Chambersburg PA
CBHW030336020726
47493CB00004B/1293